FATTY LI
DIET COOKBOOK:

Begin the Climb to Overcome your FLD - Hepatic Steatosis and Naturally Rebalance Your Metabolism for a Journey to Discover Low Fat Mouthwatering Recipes to Forget Painful Swollen | Nymph Method

SARAH ROSLIN

FATTY LIVER DIET COOKBOOK:

Copyright © 2022 by Sarah Roslin

CONTENTS

CHAPTER 1: Introduction 7

1.1 What's The Liver and His Capability? 7

1.2 What Is The Fatty Liver? 8

1.3 What Are The Sorts Of Greasy Liver Infection?.. 8

1.4 What Are The Side effects Of a Fatty Liver? 9

1.5 Why Is It Important to Treat These Issues with the Eating routine? 10

1.6 What Are The Qualities Of The No Gallbladder Diet? 11

1.7 What Is Liver Detoxification?............................... 13

1.8 What Is Cirrhosis? 14

1.9 What's Defective Stomach Disorder?................... 15

1.10 What is SIBO, or little digestive bacterial excess?16

1.11 Food Rundown: Allowed Food, Food to Stay away from..17

CHAPTER 2: FAQ 19

CHAPTER 3: SHOPPING LIST FOR A WEEK OF DIET............... 24

CHAPTER 4: MEASUREMENT CONVERSION CHART 25

CHAPTER 5: BREAKFAST RECIPES 28

5.1 Avocado Toast..28

5.2 Chickpea Omelet 28

5.3 Cinnamon Roll-Ups 29

5.4 Apple and Walnut Bread...29

5.5 Chia Pudding 30

5.6 Oatmeal Muffins 30

5.7 Blueberry Lemon Toast...31

5.8 Oatmeal Banana Pancakes.....................................31

5.9 Chickpea Pancakes..32

5.10 Pumpkin Pancakes..32

5.11 Spinach Crepes..33

5.12 Crescent Rolls..33

5.13 Scramble Tofu Toast 34

5.14 Pumpkin Bread 34

CHAPTER 6: SALADS.. 35

6.1 Greek Salad...35

6.2 Spring Salad 35

6.3 Pale Salad 36

6.4 Roasted Chickpea Salad 36

6.5 Mexican Salad...37

6.6 Beet Salad..37

6.7 Greenish Salad 38

6.8 Multi Salad 38

6.9 Sunny Salad 39

6.10 Quinoa Fruit Salad 39

6.11 Dark Salad...40

6.12 Kalpe Salad 40

CHAPTER 7: SOUPS 41

7.1 Butternut Squash Soup 41

7.2 Brussels Sprout Soup 42

7.3 Carrot Soup 42

7.4 Sweet Pea Soup 43

7.5 Cauliflower Soup 43

7.6 Golden Beet Soup 44

7.7 White Bean and Tomato Soup 44

7.8 Corn Soup 45

7.9 Mushroom Soup 45

7.10 Tomato soup 46

7.11 Pumpkin Apple Soup 47

7.12 Lentil Soup 47

CHAPTER 8: VEGETARIAN DISHES 48

8.1 Quesadillas 48

8.2 Falafel Patties 49

8.3 Penne with Spinach Sauce 49

8.4 Tomato Gazpacho 50

8.5 Chickpea Cakes 51

8.6 Red Lentils 52

8.7 Boston Baked Beans 53

8.8 Black Bean Soup 54

8.9 Meatball Sub 55

8.10 Mushroom Pot Pie 56

CHAPTER 9: VEGAN DISHES 57

9.1 Mushroom Wrap 57

9.2 Kimbap 58

9.3 Butter Squash Steak 59

9.4 Crispy Tofu with Glaze 59

9.5 Curried Black-Eyed Peas 60

9.6 Yogurt Lentil Curry With Spinach 60

9.7 Potato Gnocchi 61

9.8 Oven-Roasted Zucchini 61

9.9 Cashew Curry 62

9.10 Stuffed Cabbage 63

CHAPTER 10

FISH AND SHELLFISH 64

10.1 Cedar Planked Salmon 64

10.2 Grilled Marinated Shrimp 65

10.3 Scott Ure's Clams 65

10.4 Grilled Alaska Salmon 66

10.5 Salmon Patties 66

10.6 Garlic-Lemon Scallops 67

10.7 Steamed Mussels 67

10.8 Crab Cakes 68

10.9 Broiled Scallops 68

10.10 Oyster Stew 69

10.11 Fish Sticks 69

10.12 Fish on a Stick 70

10.13 Grilled Garlic Shrimp 70

10.14 Teriyaki Tuna Skewers 71

10.15 Tuna Kebabs with Herb Lemon, And Grains . 71

CHAPTER 11: SIDES AND SMALL PLATES 72

11.1 Cuban sandwich Sticks 72

11.2 Shrimp Skewers 72

11.3 Sesame Tuna Bites 73

11.4 Brat Skewers 73

11.5 Pizza Sticks 74

11.6 Creamy Hummus 74

11.7 Green Ranch Dip 75

11.8 French Onion Dip 75

11.9 Pesto 76

11.10 Avocado Chocolate Dip 76

CHAPTER 12: POULTRY RECIPES 77

12.1 Baked Chicken Breasts 77

12.2 Chicken Casserole 77

12.3 Chicken Pot Pie 78

12.4 Crispy Chicken Thighs 78

12.5 Chicken Tenders 79

12.6 Smoked Rotisserie Chicken 79

12.7 Peruvian Chicken Skewer 80

12.8 Bbq Chicken Skewers 81

12.9 Yucatan Chicken Grills 81

12.10 Chicken Sticks 82

12.11 Salsa Chicken Sticks 82

12.12 Grilled Teriyaki chicken cubes 83

CHAPTER 13: SNACKS AND APPETIZERS 84

13.1 Kale Chips 84

13.2 Veggie Roll-Ups 84

13.3 Edamame 85

13.4 Banana Chips 85

13.5 Apple Almond Balls 86

13.6 Rainbow Rolls 86

13.7 Crispy Sesame Cauliflower 87

13.8 Beet Chips 88

13.9 Chickpea Crackers 88

13.10 Graham Crackers 89

13.11 Crunchy Chickpeas 90

13.12 Cherry Feta Olive Salad Sticks 90

13.13 Skewered Mushrooms 91

13.14 Crispy Accordion Potatoes 91

13.15 Zucchini Rolls 92

13.16 Caprese Salad Skewers 92

13.17 Strawberry Shortcake 93

13.18 Grilled Zucchini 93

13.19 Onion Rings 94

13.20 Avocado Fries 94

CHAPTER 14: SMOOTHIES 95

14.1 Broccoli Smoothie 95

14.2 Green Smoothie 95

14.3 Pumpkin Smoothie 96

14.4 Kale Smoothie 96

14.5 Beet Smoothie 97

14.6 Spinach Smoothie 97

14.7 Celery Smoothie 98

14.8 Sweet Potato Smoothie 98

14.9 Peach Smoothie 99

14.10 Mixed Smoothie 99

14.11 Orange Smoothie 100

14.12 Raspberry Smoothie 100

14.13 Apple Smoothie 101

14.14 Choco Berry Smoothie 101

14.15 Blueberry Smoothie 102

CHAPTER 15: DRINKS 103

15.1 Chocolate Frappuccino....................103

15.2 Green Tea 103

15.3 Garlic tea..104

15.4 Lime Iced Tea..................................104

15.5 Almond coffee 105

CHAPTER 16: DESSERTS 106

16.1 Oatmeal Cookies 106

16.2 Peanut Butter Cookies 106

16.3 Pumpkin Cheesecake 107

16.4 Chocolate Mousse 108

16.5 Almond Butter Cookies...........108

16.6 Rhubarb Crunch 109

16.7 Coconut Cookies 109

16.8 Pumpkin Pie 110

16.9 Brownie Cupcakes 110

16.10 Strawberry Nice Cream 111

16.11 Meringue cookies..................111

16.12 Berry Ice Pops 112

16.13 Gingerbread Cake.................112

16.14 Churros 113

16.15 Peanut Butter Balls...............113

CHAPTER 17: 10 WEEKS MEAL PLAN 114

CHAPTER 18: CONCLUSION 124

REFERENCE PAGE 125

CHAPTER 1
INTRODUCTION

1.1 What's The Liver and His Capability?

The liver is the biggest strong organ in the human body. Various other fundamental capabilities incorporate controlling blood thickening, eliminating pollutants from the blood supply, and keeping up with stable glucose levels. Right over the rib confine in the upper mid-region, it is embedded.

Key Elements

The liver purges the blood all through the body and kills poisonous substances like liquor and opiates.

The liver secretes bile, a substance that aids processing and waste evacuation.

Four curves, each with eight divisions and a huge number of lobules, make up the liver (or little curves).

The Liver's Capabilities

The liver, A critical organ, is responsible for in excess of 500 fundamental substantial cycles. These incorporate waste and unfamiliar substance expulsion from the circulation system, glucose control, and the creation of fundamental supplements.

A protein called egg whites prevents blood from dribbling into the tissue around it. It is additionally liable for conveying nutrients, proteins, and chemicals all through the body.

For the small digestive tract to appropriately process and retain fat, bile should be created

All blood that leaves the stomach and digestive organs are cleaned by the liver of poisons, metabolites, and other possibly risky synthetics.

Amino corrosive guideline: Amino acids are expected for protein combination. The liver controls the flow's degrees of amino acids.

Vitamin K is crucial for make blood thickening coagulants, in which the liver creates a liquid called bile that is fundamental for retention.

Protection from Disease: The liver eliminates microorganisms from the circulatory system as a feature of the sifting system.

The liver has a lot of nutrients and minerals, notwithstanding iron and copper.

Additional glucose (sugar) is taken out by the liver from the circulation system and put away as glycogen. It can change glycogen back into glucose when important.

Structure of the Liver

The liver is a wedge-formed organ that is rosy brown in variety and has one restricted end over the spleen and stomach and one wide end over the small digestive system. The whole organ is housed underneath the lungs in the right upper mid-region. It's weight ranges somewhere in the range of 3 and 3.5 pounds.

Structure

The liver is comprised of four curves: caudate, quadrate, and bigger right and left curves. The falciform tendon, named after it's "sickle-molded" area on the stomach wall, isolates the left and right curves of the liver. There are a great many lobules in every one of the eight portions that make up the liver curves (little curves). The liver and the normal hepatic pipe are connected by means of a channel that goes through every one of these lobules.

Parts

A cylinder that eliminates bile from the liver is alluded to as a typical hepatic channel. It is delivered when the right and left hepatic channels meet up.

Falciform Tendon: A thin, sinewy tendon that interfaces the stomach wall to the two curves of the liver.

A layer of free connective tissue called the Glisson's case encompasses the liver and the courses and pipes along it.

The hepatic vein is the principal vein that transports oxygenated blood to the liver.

Hepatic entrance vein: A vein that transports blood from the spleen, gallbladder, pancreas, and gastrointestinal framework to the liver.

Curves: The primary components of the liver.

Lobules: Little parts that make up the liver.

Peritoneum: A layer that frames the outside of the liver.

1.2 What Is The Fatty Liver?

A lot of fat in the liver is a typical reason for hepatic steatosis, likewise alluded to as fatty liver. A limited quantity of fat in your liver is normal, yet excess can be hurtful to your well-being. A solid liver is practically without fat. At the point when fat records for 5% to 10% of your liver's weight, you have an issue.

The liver is the second-biggest organ in your body. It helps assimilation and the expulsion of hurtful substances from the blood.

A lot of fat in your liver can cause irritation and scarring. Scarring can prompt liver disappointment in serious cases.

What signs and side effects are connected with greasy liver?

A Fatty Liver Can Advance Through Four Phases:

Essentially greasy liver: There is a lot of fat in the liver. On the off chance that it doesn't deteriorate, the straightforward fatty liver is by and large protected.

Steatohepatitis: notwithstanding the abundance of fat, the liver is aroused.

Fibrosis: Scarring has come about because of persistent liver aggravation. The liver, then again, can keep on working ordinarily.

Cirrhosis: The liver every now and again creates scars, which debilitate it's capacity to work. The ongoing stage is the most obviously terrible and generally long-lasting.

1.3 What Are The Sorts Of Greasy Liver Infection?

Heavy drinker and non-alcoholic greasy liver circumstances are the two most predominant sorts.

Despite the fact that it is extraordinary, a fatty liver can happen during pregnancy.

Fatty Liver Illness Irrelevant To Liquor (NAFLD-Non Alcohlic)

Fat stores in the liver of non-weighty consumers are alluded to as non-alcoholic greasy liver illness (NAFLD).

NAFLD might be analyzed assuming you have a lot of fat in your liver and no set of experiences of weighty drinking.

Basic NAFLD is a condition where there is no irritation or different inconveniences.

NAFLD alludes to non-alcoholic steatohepatitis (NASH). It happens when aggravation and fat collection in the liver exist together. Your primary care physician might think NASH if: Your liver is unreasonably greasy.

You have an aroused liver however no set of experiences of hard-core boozing.

Without a trace of treatment, NASH can prompt liver fibrosis. Cirrhosis and liver disappointment can happen in serious cases.

Fatty Liver Illness Brought about By Liquor (AFLD-Alcoholic)

Exorbitant liquor utilization hurts the liver. The principal phase of liquor related greasy liver infection is alcoholic greasy liver illness (AFLD). Straightforward alcoholic fatty liver happens when there is no irritation or different confusions.

AFLD is exemplified by alcoholic steatohepatitis (Debris). It is otherwise called alcoholic hepatitis, and it is brought about by an abundance of fat in the liver as well as aggravation. Assuming your PCP suspects Debris, the person may

You drink a ton of liquor, your liver is excited, and you have an overflow of liver fat.

Whenever left untreated, Debris can cause liver fibrosis. Cirrhosis, extreme scarring of the liver, can prompt liver disappointment.

Acute Greasy Liver Brought about By Pregnancy (Aflppregnancy)

At the point when the liver stores an excess of fat while pregnant, the intense greasy liver of pregnancy creates (AFLP). It's an unprecedented however possibly deadly pregnancy inconvenience. Albeit the exact reason is obscure, hereditary qualities might assume a part.

AFLP for the most part shows itself during the third trimester of pregnancy. It presents serious well-being dangers to the mother and the kid whenever left untreated.

In the event that your primary care physician analyzes AFLP, it is ideal on the off chance that your child is brought into the world as quickly as time permits. You might require post pregnancy care for a couple of days subsequent to conceiving an offspring.

Inside half a month of conceiving an offspring, your liver's well-being ought to get back to business as usual.

1.4 What Are The Side effects Of a Fatty Liver?

Regularly, there are no clear side effects of a fatty liver. Then again, you could feel broken down, awkward, or in torment in your upper right stomach locale.

Liver scarring is one of the confusions that some greasy liver infection patients experience. Liver fibrosis makes the liver scar. Liver disappointment could happen on the off chance that you have cirrhosis, which has a high death rate.

Cirrhosis causes extremely durable liver harm. Along these lines, halting it before it even starts is basic.

The Following Are Signs And Side effects Of Greasy Liver:

- Stomach throb
- Diminishing craving
- Shedding pounds
- Laziness or exhaustion
- Queasiness
- Aggravation of the skin
- Yellow eyes and skin
- Promptly swelling or dying
- Dim countenances
- A light-shaded stool
- Stomach liquid development (ascites) (ascites)
- The edema or expanding in your legs

- Groups of veins under your skin that look like networks
- Expanded male bosom size
- Disarray

1.5 Why Is It Important to Treat These Issues with the Eating routine?

Dietary propensities and supplements essentially affect the beginning, course, and executives of fatty liver. A decent spot to start is with regular, natural food sources high in protein, fiber, and complex sugars. These may furnish you with dependable energy and top you off.

Whether liquor is the essential driver of greasy liver infection, the standard treatment is diet and exercise to get thinner. All in all, what are you going to eat?

As a general rule, food sources that forestall cell harm, further develop insulin use, or diminish irritation can assist with switching the condition.

Since everybody is special, you ought to talk with your PCP to foster an eating methodology that is ideal for you.

Dietary Solutions for Greasy Liver Infection

Despite the fact that it wasn't intended for individuals with greasy liver sickness, it contains food sources that assist with decreasing fat in your liver, like sound fats, cancer prevention agents, and complex starches.

On The Table, You Ought to Get The Accompanying Things:

Food things and fish

Organic products

Healthy grains

Olive oil, nuts, and vegetables

Avocados and lentils

Pick the Right Fats

Your phones utilize a sort of sugar called glucose as energy. Insulin is a chemical that works with the passage of glucose into your cells from processed food.

The greasy liver illness oftentimes prompts insulin obstruction. This implies that despite the fact that your body produces insulin, it can't as expected use it. Your blood glucose develops, and your liver transforms it into fat.

Your body's capacity to utilize insulin can be worked on by certain fats. Therefore, your liver never again needs to create and store fat, and your cells can now retain glucose.

Buy a greater amount of these:

Omega-3 unsaturated fats are found in fish, vegetable oils, fish oil, nuts (particularly pecans), flaxseeds and flaxseed oil, and verdant vegetables.

Avocados, nuts, and olives are instances of plants that are wellsprings of monounsaturated fats.

Antioxidants and Enhancements for Liver Well-being

Supplements can hurt cells in the event that they are not as expected separated. Your liver might start to collect fat therefore. Cell reinforcements, in any case, can help with safeguarding cells from this mischief. How are they obtained?

Green tea and espresso foods grew from the ground that is crude, especially berries and garlic. These incorporate sunflower seeds.

Almonds Fluid oils are gotten from plants that are high in monounsaturated unsaturated fats, similar to canola or olive oil.

Consume Minerals and Nutrients

Give the accompanying space in your eating regimen:

The vitamin D Low levels might assume a part in the movement of more serious greasy liver sickness. At the point when you are outside in the sun, your body makes vitamin D also, it is available in some dairy items. Dairy items with lower fat substance are better since they have less immersed fat.

Potassium. Low levels might be connected with non-alcoholic greasy liver infection (NAFLD). Sardines, cod, and salmon are top sources. It can likewise be found in vegetables like broccoli, peas, and yams as well as in natural products like bananas, kiwis, and apricots. Dairy items high in potassium incorporate milk and yogurt. Pick low-fat food choices.

Betaine. It could forestall greasy development in your liver, yet research discoveries are clashing. It tends to be tracked down in raw grain and shrimp.

Prior to taking any enhancements, counsel your primary care physician. They could influence the manner in which your drugs work or cause other medical problems. They probably won't work on the off chance that you don't take the right measurement in the correct way.

1.6 What Are The Qualities Of The No Gallbladder Diet?

A little organ under the liver is known as the gallbladder. To assist with fat processing, it stores liver bile.

You'll likely have to adjust your eating regimen after a medical procedure assuming you really want to have your gallbladder taken out. However much you can, you ought to attempt to avoid issues like gas, bulging, and the runs.

Subsequent to having your gallbladder taken out, there is no particular eating regimen to comply with, yet there are a few principles to follow to forestall complexities.

Avoid The Accompanying While Once again introducing Food varieties To Your Eating regimen:

- Broiled food varieties with a great deal of fat
- Food varieties with a solid fragrance
- Food varieties that cause gas

Foods to Stay away from

Subsequent to having your gallbladder taken out, you could get looseness of the bowels. Bile streams straightforwardly into your digestion tracts and fills in as a diuretic since you come up short on your gallbladder.

The Loose bowels brought about By That Interaction Commonly Disappears inside Half a month To Months. For The Best Results, Avoid These Things:

Fat-rich food sources. High-fat food sources ought to be kept away from assuming you have gas, bulging, or loose bowels after the medical procedures since they are more hard to process. By and large, your day to day calorie admission should exclude more fat than 30%. You ought to consume something like 10% of your day to day calories from soaked fat.

Pick Food sources With a Serving Size of Less Than 3g Of Fat. Food sources High in Fat Incorporate the Accompanying:

burdock root   chol i asos.

- Spread

- Meat, Pork, Sheep, and Veal

- Chicken skin Canines on a stick

- Bologna

- Cream salami

- 100 percent fat milk

- Vanilla frozen yogurt.

- Greasy cheddar

- Tropical oils incorporate palm and coconut oils.

- The handled renditions of treats, baked goods, and cakes

- Food varieties with a zesty flavor. The dynamic part in hot peppers, capsaicin, can aggravate the coating of the stomach. This might cause queasiness, regurgitating, runs, and stomach torment.

- Food sources that ordinarily exacerbate loose bowels. Staying away from food sources that are excessively sweet, high in caffeine, and dairy might help.

- Liquids to Drink Following Gallbladder Evacuation Remember that loose bowels can make your body lose liquids, nutrients, and minerals. Drink a lot of water, stock, and sports refreshments. In any case, avoid drinking for something like two days following your technique, particularly assuming you're under sedation or taking pain relievers.

- Food varieties with minimal fat: Low-fat food varieties will be more straightforward to process and will bring about less swelling, looseness of the bowels, and gas. Regardless of whether you eat low-fat food varieties after a medical procedure, you shouldn't eat over 30% of your calories from fat.

Low-fat substitutes comprise:

- Dairy items with under 1% fat or no fat

- Diminished fat cheeses

- Whites of eggs or options in contrast to eggs

- Vegetable-based burgers

- Beans, peas, and lentils

- Cereal

- Healthy grains

- Rice (brown)

- Low-fat saltines and bread

- Organic products

- Vegetables

- Soups that are vegetable-based

- Mustard

- Salsa

- Sauces made with skim milk

- Margarine (light)

- Mayonnaise (light)

- Lightweight serving of mixed greens dressings

Fiber-rich food varieties: Fiber-rich food varieties can uphold normal solid discharges. To abstain from exasperating gas and squeezing, you ought to steadily expand your fiber consumption over a time of weeks. Fiber comes in two assortments: solvent and insoluble. Both ought to be remembered for your eating routine.

During processing, Dissolvable Fiber Retains Water. It could cause expanded stools mass and slow processing. Following are a few instances of food sources high in solvent fiber:

- Dark beans
- Vegetables incorporate lima beans.
- Naval force beans
- Vegetables, pinto
- Tofu
- Chickpeas
- Soy-based burgers
- Cereal
- Avena wheat
- Apples
- Beets and Okra
- Pears
- Prunes

Insoluble fiber can't be broken down by water. It takes in fluid and sticks to different things. Gentler, greater, and more ordinary stools are the consequence of this. Insoluble fiber assists your body with handling waste. Wellsprings of insoluble fiber to search for include

- From wheat grain
- Grain wheat
- Avena grain
- Lentils beans
- Vegetables
- Berries incorporate things like strawberries, blueberries, and blackberries.
- Peas with spinach, green
- Cauliflower
- Vegetables, green
- Carrots
- Potatoes
- Nuts
- Wheat flour, the entirety

Keeping a Food Diary to Record You're Eating

To more readily comprehend what food sources mean for you in the wake of having your gallbladder eliminated, keep a food diary that incorporates the food sources you eat, the amount of them you eat, and when you eat them. Monitoring any regrettable food responses can assist you with keeping away from dangerous food sources.

1.7 What Is Liver Detoxification?

The liver fills in as the body's fundamental filtration framework, which additionally purges the blood and breaks down supplements and prescriptions to deliver a portion of the body's most urgent proteins. Keeping up with liver well-being and staying away from overindulgence is fundamental because of the liver's critical job in the body's general guideline.

A liver detox, purify, or flush is a program that makes the case that it will assist you with getting thinner, purge your collection of poisons, or in any case, work on your well-being. You need to work on your well-being inside and out. As well as purifying the collection of unsafe substances and creating bile to support absorption, the liver fills in as the body's regular detoxifier. Nearly all an individual comes into contact with can be detoxified by a good liver. On the right half of the body, the liver is arranged underneath the ribs.

The Body's Capacity To Successfully Sift Through Poisonous Substances Is Compromised When The Liver Is Debilitated. This Might Cause Various Side effects, For example,

- Tingling
- Enlarged
- Vein issues
- Yellow
- Embittered skin
- Queasiness
- Exhaustion
- Gallstones
- Looseness of the bowels

Poisons are said to gather in the liver during the separating system, as per various normal well-being experts, supplement producers, and clinical sites.

They fight that these poisons have a combined impact that can bring about many unclear side effects, serious sicknesses, and a raised gamble of malignant growth. Not much proof is places on this path.

Then again, delayed synthetic openness can hurt the liver. For example, it is notable that drinking liquor makes the liver capability decay over the long run.

The Following Are Ordinarily Remembered For A Liver Detox:

Colon and stomach purging with douches, juice fasting, liver-accommodating dietary changes, liver-accommodating enhancements, staying away from specific food sources, and the entirety of the abovementioned.

Despite the fact that liver disappointment is a serious medical problem, there is no proof that destructive poisons gather in any case sound livers without a particular openness to high centralizations of these synthetic compounds.

Clinical experts in the standard fight that liver detoxification is unsafe and pointless.

Liver Detoxification with the Eating regimen?

Dietary rules for the liver-purging eating regimen are in accordance with a decent eating routine. Slims down regularly suggest expanding the utilization of grains, water, new organic products, and vegetables, while decreasing admission of sugar, caffeine, liquor, and greasy food sources. They put extraordinary accentuation on the benefit of eating entire food varieties. Food sources that have been changed from their normal state, or handled food sources, may incorporate extra added substances and additives (like salt and sugar) (regular or manufactured synthetic compounds added to food sources to forestall ruining). Liver purifying eating regimens are an enticing momentary choice for individuals hoping to get more fit since they are normally time-restricted.

1.8 What Is Cirrhosis?

Long haul liver harm brings about cirrhosis, which is liver fibrosis or scarring. The liver can't work as expected on account of the scar tissue.

Cirrhosis is otherwise called an end-stage liver infection since it creates after prior phases of liver harm from conditions like hepatitis.

Your liver might in any case work regardless of whether you have cirrhosis. Then again, cirrhosis can ultimately bring about lethal inconveniences like a liver disappointment.

Treatment for cirrhosis could possibly prevent the condition from deteriorating.

Symptoms of Cirrhosis

You probably won't have any side effects when cirrhosis is first created.

As Your Liver turns out to be Less Solid, You Could:

I'm powerless and broken down.

I'm feeling wiped out (sick), and you don't appear to be eating.

Assuming you get in shape and muscle over the midriff, you could get red patches on your palms and little veins that seem to be bugs (bug angiomas).

Among the cirrhosis' side effects and complexities are:

Yellowing of the skin and eyes' whites (jaundice)

Swelling or draining effectively, bothersome skin in the wake of regurgitating blood, dull pee and delay crap, and enlarged legs (oedema) or stomach (ascites) because of liquid maintenance decrease in sex want (moxie)

Assuming that you figure you might have cirrhosis, address your PCP.

1.9 What's Defective Stomach Disorder?

The cracked stomach disorder is a stomach related condition that influences the coating of the digestive organs. The gastrointestinal walls have openings in the defective stomach disorder, which permits poisons and microscopic organisms to enter the circulatory system.

Regardless of being a diagnosable condition, numerous clinical experts know nothing about flawed stomach disorder (LGS). Nonetheless, the latest exploration shows that various sicknesses might be connected to the cracked stomach.

We will look at the signs, causes, and hazard variables of LGS in this article. We likewise investigate late discoveries with respect to chemical imbalance and cracked stomach. At long last, we examine potential medicines for cracked stomach and proposition guidance on the best way to further develop in general stomach well-being.

What Is A Cracked Stomach Condition, Precisely?

- The gastrointestinal (GI) lot is an organization of organs that reaches out from the mouth to the rear-end. The GI plot contains the accompanying organs:
- The midsection
- The stomach
- The digestion tracts, both little and enormous
- The supplements in food and drink are separated into more modest particles by assimilation compounds in the stomach and small digestive system, which the body can then use for energy, development, and fix.
- The digestive organs are fundamental for safeguarding the body from microorganisms and poisonous substances.
- The gastrointestinal walls have little openings that permit water and supplements to go through however not destructive substances. These openings grow in LGS, permitting poisons, microbes, and food particles to enter the circulatory system straightforwardly.

Leaky Stomach Condition and Stomach Microbiota

The stomach microbiota, a different settlement of microorganisms, likewise dwells in the digestion tracts. These microorganisms support sound resistant capability, safeguard the gastrointestinal wall and help in processing. Unbalances in the stomach's microbiota might be the reason for LGS.

Unbalances in the stomach microbiota can make the resistant framework become dynamic, as per a recent report. Because of this, penetrability and digestive aggravation are expanded (IP). IP alludes to how effectively substances can enter the circulatory system from the digestion tracts.

- The condition is known as IBS (IBS)
- Celiac disease
- Celiac sickness
- Industrious hepatitis
- Diabetes
- Food responsive qualities and sensitivities
- Polycystic ovary disorder (PCOS)

It is as yet indistinct whether LGS reflects or adds to these diseases.

A 2015 survey article from Believed Source guarantees that raised IP might affect the beginning of fiery entrails infection (IBD). IP was found in a recent report before the beginning of type 1 diabetes.

Uneasiness and wretchedness are two emotional wellness conditions that might be affected by the flawed stomach disorder. Regardless, more exploration is expected to back up this case.

Symptoms

A large number of the broken stomach disorder's side effects are likewise present in other ailments. Specialists might experience issues diagnosing the illness thus.

A Defective Stomach Might Add To or Worsen the Accompanying Side effects:

- Throbbing joints
- Swelling
- Disarray
- Clogging
- Broad provocative response
- Exhaustion
- Cerebral pains
- Supplement deficiencies
- Issues focusing
- Consistently encountering loose bowels
- Skin issues incorporate dermatitis, rashes, and skin inflammation.

1.10 What is SIBO, or little digestive bacterial excess?

SIBO represents little gastrointestinal bacterial abundance.

A shorthand for "little digestive bacterial excess" is SIBO. It demonstrates that the frameworks liable for holding the equilibrium of your stomach vegetation under control aren't working and that the microbes in your small digestive tract have duplicated. Albeit the small digestive tract harbors various solid and typical microscopic organisms, an abundance of some unacceptable ones can prompt stomach related issues. Some unacceptable microscopic organisms can stifle the essential valuable microbes and upset your stomach related framework by brushing on food varieties that aren't appropriate for them.

What Outcomes in SIBO?

Your body utilizes a perplexing organization of compound and mechanical cycles to control the greenery in your stomach. Assuming at least one of these instruments breakdown, SIBO might create. Gastric corrosive, bile, chemicals, and immunoglobulins are a couple of the substances that the small digestive system uses to direct the microbes that lives there. These synthetic cycles can be prevented by various elements. Another vital purifying interaction is the entry of food from the small digestive tract into the internal organ. On the off chance that this framework dials back or separates, microorganisms in the digestive organ might begin to move up, giving the microbes in the small digestive tract additional opportunity to create.

What Impacts Does SIBO Have On My Body?

Microorganisms convert sugars into gas and short-chain unsaturated fats in the small digestive tract. Expanded bacterial includes could bring about additional gas and different side-effects, which could cause loose bowels. The microscopic organisms additionally consume proteins, vitamin B12, and bile salts, which are accepted to help with the muscle to fat ratio's utilization. These variables add to lacking mineral and fat-solvent nutrient retention as well as unfortunate fat absorption. This has an assortment of short-and long haul gastrointestinal impacts, including a lack of healthy sustenance. Shortages in nutrients and minerals after some time could hurt your bones and sensory system.

Is SIBO Far reaching?

Up to 80% of individuals with crabby inside condition (IBS) have SIBO, per a few investigations. Obscure among solid people is the commonness. As indicated by doctors, SIBO is every now and again misdiagnosed. Gentle cases may not show any side effects, but rather moderate cases display a large number of summed up side effects similar to those seen in different diseases like IBS. SIBO is seldom tried unequivocally, and when it is, the methodology used are deficient.

Symptoms

SIBO much of the time results from another ailment and has comparative signs and side effects to other gastrointestinal circumstances.

- Stomach augmentation
- A stomach torment
- Bulging
- Stoppage
- The runs

- Weakness
- Gas
- Heartburn
- Deficiency of weight that wasn't expected
- Queasiness

1.11 Food Rundown: Allowed Food, Food to Stay away from

Permitted Food varieties

- Almonds
- Almonds
- Apples
- Artichokes
- Arugula
- Avocados
- Beets
- Berries
- Berries
- Broccoli
- Brussels sprouts
- Cabbage
- Canola oil
- Carrots
- Cauliflower
- Chia seeds
- Espresso
- Dandelion
- Fish and fish
- Flaxseed

- Organic products
- Goji berry
- Grapefruit
- Green tea
- Greens
- Indian gooseberry
- Vegetables
- Lemons
- Licorice root
- Limes
- Low fat dairy
- Milk thorn
- Olive oil
- Olives
- Onions
- Papaya
- Peanuts
- Peas
- Raw garlic
- Raw honey

- Red chime peppers
- Salmon
- Sardines
- Soy or whey protein
- Spinach
- Sunflower seeds

- Yams
- Tomatoes
- Turmeric
- Pecans
- Pecans
- Entire grains

Foods to Keep away from

- Liquor
- Bacon
- Prepared products
- Spread
- Restored meats
- Greasy meats
- Seared food varieties
- Full-fat cheddar
- Ghee
- Low calorie diet drinks
- Meat
- Palm or coconut oils
- Poultry, aside from lean white meat
- Handled
- Red meat
- Refined grains
- Pungent food varieties
- Wiener
- Pop
- Sugar and added sugars

- Sweet refreshments
- White bread
- White pasta
- White rice
- Yogurt, with the exception of low-fat

CHAPTER 2

FAQ

1. What Food sources should you remember for a Solid Liver Eating regimen?

A. Coffee: Espresso can help with the decrease of strange liver chemicals.

Greens: Greens help to keep fat under control.

Soy and beans: To diminish the gamble of NAFLD, consume beans and soy.

Fish: Fish can assist with bringing down aggravation and fat levels.

Cereal: Oats are high in fiber.

Nuts: Nuts can assist with irritation decrease.

Turmeric: There is proof that turmeric brings down liver harm pointers.

Sunflower seeds: Sunflower seeds are high in cancer prevention agents.

Unsaturated fats: Increment your admission of unsaturated fats.

Garlic: Garlic has been displayed to work on generally speaking well-being.

2. What dietary and way of life suggestions are there to invert greasy liver illness?

A. Whether or not liquor assumes a part, the standard treatment for greasy liver sickness is to shed   pounds through diet and exercise. All in all, what would it be a good idea for you to eat?

By and large, food sources that forestall cell harm, further develop insulin usage, or lessen aggravation can help with the recuperation of the condition.

Since every individual is one of a kind, you ought to work with your primary care physician to foster an eating methodology that is ideal for you.

3. How can greasy liver fix normally?

- A. Natural cures
- Lose overabundance weight
- Practice good eating habits
- Drink espresso
- Get dynamic
- Keep away from added sugars
- Decrease cholesterol
- Omega-3s
- Keep away from known liver aggravations
- Get some information about vitamin E

- Research spices

4. Is greasy liver a difficult condition?

A. The driving reason for the normal condition known as greasy liver condition is the gathering of additional fat in the liver. Most of the individuals experience no side effects and no critical issues subsequently. Notwithstanding, it can every so often cause liver harm. The great news is that greasy liver illness can frequently be forestalled or even relieved by changing your way of life.

5. What is the system of greasy liver illness?

A. The following are conceivable pathophysiologic systems for greasy liver: diminished unsaturated fat beta-oxidation in the mitochondria worked on unsaturated fat conveyance to the liver or expanded endogenous unsaturated fat blend. It is hard to consolidate or send out fatty oils as exceptionally low-thickness lipoprotein.

6. How could I at any point distinguish in the event that am having a greasy liver?

A. Imaging techniques

A sensation of completion or torment in the upper right half of the midsection (tummy).

Queasiness, loss of craving, or weight reduction

The skin is yellowish, similar to the whites of the eyes (jaundice).

Enlarged legs and midsection (edema).

Extreme sleepiness or disarray in the brain

Shortcoming.

7. How extreme is a grade 3 greasy liver?

A. Grade 3 greasy liver is certainly not a difficult condition without help from anyone else. In any case, quite possibly it could hurt somebody.

8. What are the best activities for greasy liver?

A. Resistance or strength preparing activities, for example, weightlifting can likewise assist with greasy liver sickness. Go for the gold minutes of moderate to incredible oxygen consuming activity five days every week and three days of moderate to energetic strength preparing.

9. Can Liv.52 fix greasy liver?

A. It has been shown that LIV 52 assists patients with liver harm, particularly those with alcoholic steatosis and emotional and clinical boundaries. The outcome is irrefutably inferable from better dietary and way of life decisions as well as expanded patient inspiration.

10. Does greasy a liver transform into cirrhosis?

A. Some NAFLD patients might encounter the movement of non-alcoholic steatohepatitis (NASH), an extreme type of the greasy liver infection portrayed by a liver irritation, prompting progressed scarring (cirrhosis) and liver disappointment.

11. What nutrient assists with a greasy liver?

A. Vitamins A, B3, B12, D, and E can be generally used to treat NAFLD, however some have been connected to aftereffects.

12. Can a grade 1 greasy liver be switched?

A. If you make the vital dietary changes and work out something like five times each week, grade I greasy liver can be switched.

13. What is greasy liver illness?

A. A condition known as greasy liver illness is gotten on by a lot of fat the liver. A sound liver contains practically no fat. An issue emerges when fat makes up 5% to 10% of the heaviness of your liver.

14. How quick might greasy liver at any point be restored?

A.It is feasible to fix greasy liver illness. Following fourteen days of forbearance from liquor, your liver ought to work typically again.

15. Can a non-alcoholic greasy liver be switched?

A. There may be a hereditary part that is challenging to treat. Basically, it runs in certain individuals' qualities. Like pancreatitis, viral contamination might be the foundation of it. Just take the most ideal consideration of your overall wellbeing to recuperate from the episode.

Instinctive fat and liquor utilization would diminish on the off chance that it were a slow condition that arose over the long haul. Any bacterial or viral diseases that might be influencing your body or liver ought to be dealt with. (For example, chemotherapy for Hepatitis C) When contrasted with an expected liver transfer, which requires immunosuppressive prescriptions and isn't a choice in the event that you have a likely liver sickness yet ought to be kept away from please, a few viral diseases cost huge amount of cash to treat and can require as long as 9 months to fix.

Without a natural reason, it very well may be a hereditary inclination. To decide the best clinical course to follow and the best tests to run, talk with a hepatologist, or liver trained professional, about your specific condition. They will actually want to encourage you on the ideal clinical trials to direct.

This isn't clinical guidance; rather, it's an idea that you talk with specialists to decide the best course of treatment for your condition.

16. How might I at any point determine what stage my greasy liver is ready?

A. Diagnoses and Tests

Utilize registered tomography or ultrasound to make an image of the liver (CT check).

A liver biopsy is utilized to decide the seriousness of the liver sickness (tissue test).

To gauge how much fat and scar tissue in the liver, a specific ultrasound called a fibroscan is in some cases utilized rather than a liver biopsy.

17. How long does it take to foster a greasy liver?

A. An unreasonable measure of fat in the liver welcomed on by consuming such a large number of calories while carrying on with a stationary way of life for a drawn out timeframe is known as greasy liver.

Put your body in a calorie-lacking mode to lose no less than 7-10% of your body weight, which will rely heavily on the amount of your circumferences a portion of your level in centimeters.

You want to get more fit step by step, not by sticking to an accident diet.

Roughly 7000 calories make up 1 kg.

Consequently, you should consume a sum of 49000 calories, which you partition by days to show up at the ideal number, to lose 7 kg of weight.

Consider the situation where you want to cut your everyday caloric admission by 490 calories in only 100 days. To safeguard yourself, put forth an objective of cutting your day to day caloric admission by 245 calories in 200 days, which your body can endure and won't cause you to feel denied.

Your eating regimen ought to comprise of 80% of low-calorie foods grown from the ground, like salad greens, and 20% grains like heartbeats, curds, and kidney beans.

18. How numerous years can a human live with greasy liver?

A. Fatty liver is a typical difficulty for individuals who are overweight/drink extreme liquor/have an undesirable eating regimen with a satiate of soaked fat/stay alive on bundled low quality food/inclined are to a stationary way of life with little activity.

Many individuals are logical ignorant they have a greasy liver except if a USG is performed.

Gentle greasy liver is reversible with few way of life changes/abandoning extreme liquor utilization. Drug additionally makes a difference.

Ignoring it can, in any case, be perilous. Greasy liver, past a phase, can bring about intense liver sickness, which is dangerous.

19. Who has a greasy liver sickness? /What are the reasons for greasy liver?

A. Fatty liver infection is the most predominant sort of liver illness around the world. At the point when we allude to greasy liver illness as a general rule, we mean Non-Alcoholic Greasy Liver Sickness despite the fact that it tends to be welcomed by various things, like liquor, Wilson's infection, other metabolic liver illnesses, and different medications.

Here is a rundown of individuals who are in danger of creating greasy liver illness in the event that you're pondering who has it.

The metabolic disorder is characterized by stomach stoutness in addition to any two of the accompanying side effects: Fatty substances of 150 mg/dL (or utilizing medicine to treat this hazard factor), HDL cholesterol of 40 mg/dL in men and 50 mg/dL in ladies, and fasting glucose of in excess of 100 mg/dL.

Diabetes type 2 mellitus

Polycystic ovary disorder welcomed by persistent hepatitis C infection disease (PCOS)

Obstructive Rest Apnea Problem Medical procedure for the Gastrointestinal Plot that Is Incredibly Troublesome

Glucocorticoids, nifedipine, trimethoprim/sulfamethoxazole, tamoxifen, manufactured estrogens, chloroquine, irinotecan, oxaliplatin, and different drugs, including amiodarone.

Coordinated Parenteral Nourishment (TPN).

Albeit the previously mentioned causes are speculative, having diabetes, being overweight, or being large expands your gamble of creating a greasy liver condition.

PS. Greasy liver and greasy liver condition are not exactly the same things. There are different kinds of a greasy liver. The beginning of greasy liver is the development of fat in liver cells. This gentle steatosis can be exacerbated by fibrosis and fiery changes in the liver (steatohepatitis), bringing about cirrhosis of the liver and, sometimes, hepatocellular carcinoma. Subsequently, we possibly group somebody as having a sickness when they experience harm, including irritation or potentially fibrosis.

20. Does a greasy liver hurt?

A. The greasy liver infection regularly causes no side effects until the sickness advances to cirrhosis of the liver. On the off chance that you really do encounter any side effects, they may be upper right stomach torment or a sensation of totality (midsection). Albeit greasy liver illness seldom causes side effects, it is a significant admonition sign that you are drinking exorbitantly. Greasy liver infection can be turned around. Your liver ought to get back to business as usual following fourteen days of not drinking liquor.

CHAPTER 3
SHOPPING LIST FOR A WEEK OF DIET

Quantity	Quantity in units
½ lime	44g lime
½ cucumber	150g cucumber
½ cup fresh spinach	64g fresh spinach
1 ½ green apples	225g green apples
1 ¾ lemon	101.5g lemon
1 beets	110g beets
1 cups fresh pineapple chunks	210g fresh pineapple chunks
1 inch piece fresh ginger	7g inch piece fresh ginger
12 carrots	2 ½ carrots
3 ½ leaves kale	7 oz. leaves kale
3 apples	450g apple
3 organic oranges	420g organic oranges
4 stalks celery	160g stalks celery

CHAPTER 4
MEASUREMENT CONVERSION CHART

Weight

Imperial	Mertic (Approximate)
½ oz.	15 g
1 oz.	30 g
2 oz.	60g
3 oz.	90 g
4oz.	125g
6 oz.	175g
8 oz.	250g
10 oz.	300g
12 oz.	375 g
13 oz.	400 g
14 oz.	425 g
1 lb	500 g
1½ lb	750 g
2lb	1 kg

Liquid Measures

Quantity	Mertic (Approximate)
1 teaspoon	5ml
1 tablespoon	15 ml
¼ cup	60 ml
1/3 cup	80 ml
½ cup	125 ml
1 cup	250 ml
1-¼ cup	300 ml
1½ cup	375 ml
1-2/3 cup	400 ml
1¾ cup	450 ml
2 cups	500 ml
2½ cups	600 ml
3 cups	750 ml

LEGEND

Serves Plate

Preparation Time Clock

Cooking Time Pot

Nutrition Facts

Ingredients Full Cart

Procedure Book

Calories

Total Fat

Protien

Total Carbohydrate

Dietary Fiber

Sugar

Sodium

Cholesterol

Total Energy

CHAPTER 5

BREAKFAST RECIPES

5.1 Avocado Toast

| per serving | 395 Cal | 26.6g | 34.7g | 10.6g | 9g | 1347 mg | 369 mg |

- Black pepper - ⅛ tsp.
- Chili flakes - ⅛ tsp.
- Salt - ⅛ tsp.
- Parsley sprigs - 2
- Toast, whole grain - 2 piece
- Cream cheese - 4 tbsp.
- Tomatoes, sun-dried - 4
- Avocado slices - 8

1. Spread cream cheese evenly on both toasts.
2. On each toast, place 4 avocado slices.
3. Distribute the parsley springs evenly on each toast.
4. On each toast, place 2 sun-dried tomatoes.
5. Season with salt, pepper, and chili flakes before serving.

Leftover recipe storage: Store in the container and cover it with lid, place the container in the refrigerator.

Leftover recipe reheat/reuse instructions: Take the desired quantity from the refrigerator, heat in the microwave or on a pan and serve.

5.2 Chickpea Omelet

| per serving | 220 Cal | 9.3g | 27.7g | 9.7g | 9g | 1014 mg | 385 mg |

- Baking soda - ½ tsp.
- Black pepper - ¼ tsp.
- Cherry tomatoes, cut in half - 4
- Chickpea flour - 1 cup
- Garlic powder - ½ tsp.
- Green onions, chopped - 3
- Green seedlings - 1 bunch
- Nutritional yeast - 1/3 cup
- Onion powder - ½ tsp.
- White pepper - ¼ tsp.

1. Combine onion flour, garlic powder, chickpea powder, white pepper, black pepper, baking soda, and nutritional yeast in a mixing bowl.
2. The mixture needs to be smoothed out with the addition of 1 cup of water.
3. Melt the butter in a medium saucepan over medium heat. Fill the heating pan with batter halfway. Cook after including green onions and mushrooms to the batter. After 3 to 5 minutes, flip the omelet when the top is done. When the omelet's top side is done, flip it over and let it cook for an additional one to two minutes.
4. With seedlings and cherry tomatoes on top, fold the omelet and serve it hot.

Leftover recipe storage: Store in the container and cover it with lid, place the container in the refrigerator.

Leftover recipe reheat/reuse instructions: Take the desired quantity from the refrigerator, heat in the microwave or on a pan and serve.

5.3 Cinnamon Roll-Ups

| per serving | 110 Cal | 5g | 12g | 0g | 7.2g | 34 mg | 15 mg |

- Crescent rolls - ½ package
- Sugar - ⅛ cup
- Ground cinnamon - ½ tbsp.
- Thick wood sticks - 8

1. Mix together the sugar and ground cinnamon in a small bowl.
2. With a knife cut the crescent rolls in half and wrap them around the wood sticks.
3. Roll them in the sugar-cinnamon mixture.
4. Cook for about 5 minutes while rotating over the campfire.
5. Garnish with white glaze, honey, or maple syrup, if desired.

Leftover recipe storage: Store in the container and cover it with lid, place the container in the refrigerator.

Leftover recipe reheat/reuse instructions: Take the desired quantity from the refrigerator, heat in the microwave or on a pan and serve.

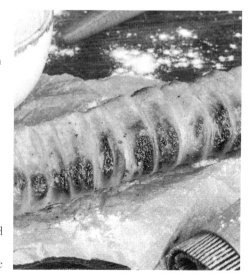

5.4 Apple and Walnut Bread

| per serving | 293 Cal | 5.4g | 57.6g | 5.6g | 30.3g | 259 mg | 465 mg |

- Applesauce, unsweetened - 1½ cups
- Baking powder - ½ tsp.
- Baking soda - 1 tsp.
- Chopped walnuts - ½ cup
- Cinnamon, ground - 1 tsp.
- Ground flax seeds - 1 tbsp. (mixed with 2 tbsp. Warm water)
- Light brown sugar - ¾ cup
- Plant milk, unsweetened - 1/3 cup
- Salt - 1 tsp.
- Whole wheat flour - 2 cups

1. Put the temperature of the oven to 375 degrees Fahrenheit.
2. Mix the applesauce, brown sugar, almond milk, and flax seed mixture in a large bowl. Set aside.
3. In a different medium bowl, mix together the flour, baking soda, baking powder, salt, and cinnamon.
4. The dry ingredients need to be mixed in well with the wet ones. Stir in the walnuts.
5. When you pour the batter into the 9x5-inch loaf pan, spread it out evenly.
6. Take out of the pan and let cool on a wire rack for a full hour before serving. Bake for 28 minutes, or until golden brown and a toothpick inserted in the middle comes out clean.

Leftover recipe storage: Store in the container and cover it with lid, place the container in the refrigerator.

Leftover recipe reheat/reuse instructions: Take desired quantity from the container and serve.

5.5 Chia Pudding

| per serving | 171 Cal | 7.1g | 24.2g | 3.7g | 14.9g | 267 mg | 153 mg |

- Chia seeds - ½ cup
- Vanilla extract - ½ tsp.
- Almond milk unsweetened - 1 cup
- Pure maple syrup - 1 tbsp.
- Raspberries, for topping - ¼ cup

1. Mix the almond milk, chia seeds, vanilla, and syrup together in a medium bowl.
2. Before you serve it, put the bowl in the fridge for at least 30 minutes or overnight.

Leftover recipe storage: Store in the container and cover it with lid, place the container in the refrigerator.

Leftover recipe reheat/reuse instructions: Take desired quantity from the container and serve.

5.6 Oatmeal Muffins

| per serving | 193 Cal | 8.7g | 26.4g | 4.9g | 11.3g | 262 mg | 72 mg |

- Ground flaxseed - ¼ cup (mix in ½ cup hot water for 5 minutes)
- Maple syrup - ¼ cup
- Baking soda - ¼ tsp.
- Sea salt - ¼ tsp.
- Almond milk - ½ cup
- Raisins - ½ cup
- Walnuts -
- Apple, chopped - 1
- Banana, sliced - 1
- Rolled oats - 2 cups
- Cinnamon - 2 tbsp.
- Peanuts for serving - ¼ cup

1. Use muffin liners to line a 12-cup muffin pan.
2. Put all of the muffin ingredients in a food processor and pulse for 30 seconds, or until everything is mixed but not smooth.
3. Divide the batter among the cupcake liners in an even layer.
4. Bake for 20 minutes at 350°F.
5. Sprinkle with peanuts before serving.

Leftover recipe storage: Store in the container and cover it with lid, place the container in the refrigerator.

Leftover recipe reheat/reuse instructions: Take desired quantity from the container and serve.

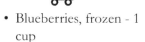

- Blueberries, frozen - 1 cup
- Bread slices, whole grain - 6
- Cinnamon - 1 tsp.
- Ground flaxseed- 2 tbsp. (mix in ¼ cup hot water for 5 minutes)
- Lemon, juice - ½
- Maple syrup - 1-2 tbsp.
- Nutmeg - ½ tsp.
- Plant-based milk - 1 cup
- Sea salt - ⅛ tsp.
- Vanilla extract - 1 tsp.

1. Mix the spices, salt, and vanilla extract together in a large bowl.

2. Combine the spice mixture, flax mixture, and plant-based milk in a mixing bowl.

3. Preheat the nonstick skillet on low heat.

4. Soak the bread in a mixture of milk and eggs. Cook the bread slices in a nonstick skillet until crispy, then flip and brown the other side.

5. In the meantime, mix the lemon juice, blueberries, and maple syrup in a medium bowl that can go in the microwave. Stir, and microwave for 3–7 minutes, or until smooth and mixed.

6. Drizzle with blueberry syrup and serve once both sides of the toast are crispy.

Leftover recipe storage: Store in the container and cover it with lid, place the container in the refrigerator.

Leftover recipe reheat/reuse instructions: Take the desired quantity from the refrigerator, heat in the microwave or on a pan and serve.

- Oats, gluten-free - 1 ½ cups
- Plant-based milk, unsweetened - 1 cup
- Cinnamon - 1 tsp.
- Sea salt - ⅛ tsp.
- Ripe bananas - 3
- Chia seeds - 3 tbsp.
- Dates - 6

1. Mix 1 cup of oats, plant-based milk, chia seeds, dates, 2 bananas, cinnamon, and sea salt in a food processor. Pulse for 1 to 3 minutes, or until the mixture is smooth.

2. Then add the rest of the oats and banana and mix well.

3. The pan should be heated on medium-low heat.

4. Pour the batter in and let it cook until you see a bubble on the bottom. Cook the pancake for another 2–3 minutes, or until it is done. Cook the pancakes until there is no more batter.

5. If desired, serve hot with your favorite sauce.

Leftover recipe storage: Store in the container and cover it with lid, place the container in the refrigerator.

Leftover recipe reheat/reuse instructions: Take the desired quantity from the refrigerator, heat in the microwave or on a pan and serve.

5.9 Chickpea Pancakes

per serving	89 Cal	1.2g	15.6g	4.5g	1g	83 mg	122 mg

- Paprika - ¼ tsp.
- Carrot, shredded - ½ cup
- Garbanzo flour - ½ cup
- Water - ½ cup
- Baking soda - ¼ tsp.
- Small garlic clove, minced - 1

1. In a large mixing bowl, combine all of the pancake ingredients.

2. Heat the pan over a medium-low flame.

3. Pour in the batter and cook until bubbles form on the bottom.

4. Cook the other side for about two to three minutes, or until the pancake is done. Cook the pancakes until the batter is finished.

5. If desired, serve with your favorite sauce.

Leftover recipe storage: Store in the container and cover it with lid, place the container in the refrigerator.

Leftover recipe reheat/reuse instructions: Take the desired quantity from the refrigerator, heat in the microwave or on a pan and serve.

5.10 Pumpkin Pancakes

per serving	555 Cal	12.7g	100.9 g	9.6g	34.5g	1467 mg	1162 mg

- Unsweetened almond milk - 1 ¼ cups
- 100% pumpkin puree - ½ heaping cup
- Canola oil - 1-2 tbsp.
- Spelt flour - 1 ¼ cups
- Vanilla extract - 1 tsp.
- Baking powder - 2 tsp.
- Organic cane sugar - 3 tbsp.
- Pumpkin pie spice or cinnamon - ¾ tsp.
- Salt - 1 pinch
- Pure maple syrup - for serving

1. Heat the griddle to the temperature suggested by the manufacturer, which for pancakes is usually 350 degrees. Heat a stovetop griddle/skillet over medium heat. To keep the pancakes warm, heat the oven to 200°F and put a cookie sheet on the middle rack while it heats up.

2. In a medium-sized bowl, mix the flour, sugar, baking powder, and spices well. Combine well after adding the pumpkin puree, vanilla, and nondairy milk.

3. Put enough oil on the griddle or pan to cover it. Use a 14-cup measure to scoop out the batter and put it on the griddle. Give it about three minutes to cook, or until the edges start to bubble and look leathery. Then flip it and cook it for 3 more minutes. Keep adding oil to the griddle or skillet until there is no more batter.

4. Garnish with pure maple syrup. 2 tbsp. chopped pecans on top adds protein and texture.

Leftover recipe storage: Store in the container and cover it with lid, place the container in the refrigerator.

Leftover recipe reheat/reuse instructions: Take the desired quantity from the refrigerator, heat in the microwave or on a pan and serve.

5.11 Spinach Crepes

per serving	271 Cal	6.9g	44g	9g	7.8g	641 mg	163 mg

- Cherry tomatoes - 4-6
- Soy milk - 1 cup
- Spinach - 2 cups
- Plain flour - 1 cup
- Baby spinach - ⅛ cup
- Salt - ⅛ tsp.
- Canola oil, for cooking

1. Mix all of the crepe ingredients in a blender until they are smooth.
2. Warm a large skillet over medium-low heat.
3. Add a small amount of oil to the pan.
4. When the oil is hot, put a little batter in the middle of the pan and lift and tilt it to spread the batter out evenly.
5. When the crepe's top is done, use a spatula to loosen it and flip it over.
6. Cook for about 1-2 minutes is enough time for the other side to get a light brown color.
7. Then, with the remaining batter, repeat until finished.
8. Crepes should be served with baby spinach and cherry tomatoes.

Leftover recipe storage: Store in the container and cover it with lid, place the container in the refrigerator.

Leftover recipe reheat/reuse instructions: Take the desired quantity from the refrigerator, heat in the microwave or on a pan and serve.

5.12 Crescent Rolls

per serving	42 Cal	1.2g	7.5g	0.7g	2.3g	12 mg	78 mg

- All-purpose flour - for surface
- All-purpose baking mix - 3-3 ½ cups
- Envelope active dry yeast - 1 ¼ -oz.
- Sugar - 2 tbsp.
- Warm water - ¾ cup

1. Mix the yeast and warm water in a 1-cup measuring cup and set it aside for 5 minutes. In a large bowl, stir together 3 cups of baking mix, sugar, and yeast mixture while stirring.
2. Turn the dough out onto a lightly floured surface and knead until smooth and elastic, adding up to ½ cup more baking mix if needed (about 10 minutes).
3. Roll the dough into a circle that is ½ inches across, and then cut it in half. Roll the wedges into crescent shapes, beginning at the wide end. Put the crescents, pointy sides down, on a large, lightly greased baking sheet. Cover and put in a warm (85°) place without drafts for an hour, or until the volume has doubled.
4. Set the oven to 425°F and bake for 10–12 minutes, or until golden brown.

Leftover recipe storage: Store in an airtight container.

Leftover recipe reheat/reuse instructions: Take desired quantity from the container and serve.

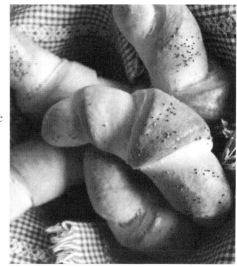

5.13 Scramble Tofu Toast

per serving	638 Cal	49g	33.4g	30.1g	10.6g	1789 mg	185 mg

- Almond milk - 1/3 cup
- Avocado, mashed - 1
- Cherry tomatoes - 4
- Diced yellow onion - ½ cup
- Dijon mustard - ½ tsp.
- Extra-virgin olive oil - 1 tbsp.
- Extra-firm tofu (patted dry and crumbled) - 14 ounces
- Freshly ground black pepper - ⅛ tsp.
- Garlic cloves, minced - 2
- Ground cumin - ¼ tsp.
- Ground turmeric - ¼ tsp.
- Nutritional yeast - 2 tbsp.
- Sea salt - ⅛ tsp.
- Spinach - ½ cup

1. Mix the almond milk, nutritional yeast, garlic, mustard, turmeric, cumin, and ½ tsp. salt together in a small bowl. Place aside.
2. In a large saucepan, heat the oil over medium heat. Cook for about 5 minutes, or until the onion is soft, adding salt and pepper.
3. Next, add the tofu and cook it for 3–5 minutes, or until it is fully heated. Turn the heat down to low, and while stirring, add the almond milk mixture. About 3 minutes, stirring occasionally. Add black pepper that has been freshly ground to taste.
4. Toast the slices of bread.
5. On each toast, spread the mashed avocado.
6. Spread the tofu evenly on both toasts.
7. Serve with spinach and cherry tomatoes.

Leftover recipe storage: Store in the container and cover it with lid, place the container in the refrigerator.

Leftover recipe reheat/reuse instructions: Take the desired quantity from the refrigerator, heat in the microwave or on a pan and serve.

5.14 Pumpkin Bread

per serving	232 Cal	4g	47g	4g	24g	182 mg	185 mg

- All-purpose flour - 2 cups
- Ginger ground - ½ tsp.
- Baking powder - 1 ½ tsp.
- Bananas, mashed - 1 cup
- Brown sugar - 1 cup
- Cinnamon ground - ½ tsp.
- Pecans, chopped - ½ cup
- Pumpkin pie spice, ground - ½ tsp.
- Pumpkin puree, canned - 1 cup
- Baking soda - ½ tsp.
- Pumpkin seeds - ¼ cup
- Salt - ¼ tsp.

1. Set the temperature of the oven to 350°F.
2. Set aside an 8-inch-long piece of parchment paper and a loaf pan.
3. In a large bowl, stir together the flour, baking powder, baking soda, salt, cinnamon, ginger powder, pumpkin pie spice, and nutmeg.
4. In a separate large bowl, mix the pumpkin puree, brown sugar, and mashed bananas.
5. Mix the wet and dry ingredients together with a spatula until they are well blended. Fold in ¼ cup of pecans.
6. Half-fill a loaf pan with the bread mixture, and then sprinkle the rest of the pecans and pumpkin seeds on top.
7. Bake for 50–70 minutes, or until a toothpick stuck in the middle comes out clean.
8. Let it cool for 10–15 minutes, then move it to a cooling rack to finish cooling.
9. Serve with spread or jam, if you like.

Leftover recipe storage: Store in the container and cover it with lid, place the container in the refrigerator.

Leftover recipe reheat/reuse instructions: Take the desire quantity from the refrigerator, and serve warm or cold.

CHAPTER 6

SALADS

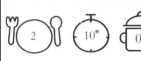

6.1 Greek Salad

per serving	211 Cal	11.1g	25.8g	7.2g	13.1g	1044 mg	317 mg

- Salad
- Baby spinach - ¼ cup
- Cherry tomatoes, halved - 4
- Cucumber, lengthwise sliced - 1
- Medium red onion, sliced - 1
- Olives – 6-8
- Parsley - ¼ cup
- Plant-based ricotta cheese, cubed - 3 tbsp.
- Yellow bell pepper, sliced - ½
- Dressing
- Extra virgin olive oil - 1 tbsp.
- Lemon - 1 tbsp.
- Pepper - ⅛ tsp.
- Salt - ⅛ tsp.

1. Combine all of the salad ingredients in a large bowl.
2. Dressing ingredients should be combined in a small bowl.
3. To get an even coating, toss the salad mix with the ingredients for the dressing.
4. Put the salad on a serving dish and serve.

Leftover recipe storage: Store in a bowl and cover it with a lid, and place the bowl in the refrigerator.

Leftover recipe reheat/reuse instructions: Take the desired quantity from the bowl and serve.

6.2 Spring Salad

per serving	293 Cal	17.8g	34.6g	5.5g	22g	1411 mg	34 mg

- Salad
- Cucumber, sliced - 1
- Avocado, sliced - ½
- Red radishes, sliced - 3
- Lettuce leaves - 1 bunch
- Cherry tomatoes, halved - 4-6
- Dressing
- Extra virgin olive oil - 1 tbsp.
- Traditional balsamic glaze - 2 tbsp.
- Spring onions - 2-3 tbsp.

1. Combine all of the salad ingredients in a large bowl.
2. Dressing ingredients should be combined in a small bowl.
3. To get an even coating, toss the salad mix with the ingredients for the dressing.
4. Put the salad on a serving dish and serve.

Leftover recipe storage: Store in a bowl and cover it with a lid, and place the bowl in the refrigerator.

Leftover recipe reheat/reuse instructions: Take the desired quantity from the bowl and serve.

6.3 Pale Salad

per serving	306 Cal	12.6g	40g	14.1g	18.8g	1283 mg	594 mg

- Salad
- Baby spinach - ½ cup
- Cherry tomatoes, halved – 6-8
- Large cucumber, sliced - 1
- Lettuce leaves - 1 bunch
- Medium onion, sliced - 1
- Yellow bell pepper, sliced - ½
- Dressing
- Salt - ¼ tsp.
- Black sesame seeds - ½ tsp.
- Extra virgin olive oil - 1 tbsp.
- Paprika - ⅛ tsp.
- White sesame seeds - ½ tsp.
- Pepper - ⅛ tsp.

1. Combine all of the salad ingredients in a large bowl.
2. Dressing ingredients should be combined in a small bowl.
3. To get an even coating, toss the salad mix with the ingredients for the dressing.
4. Put the salad on a serving dish and serve.

Leftover recipe storage: Store in a bowl and cover it with a lid, and place the bowl in the refrigerator.

Leftover recipe reheat/reuse instructions: Take the desired quantity from the bowl and serve.

6.4 Roasted Chickpea Salad

per serving	611 Cal	34.3g	65.3g	17g	10.3g	1411 mg	1425 mg

- Salad
- White pepper - ⅛ tsp.
- Roasted chickpeas - 1 cup
- Avocado, sliced - 1
- Parsley - 1 cup
- Lemon wedges - 2
- Cherry tomatoes, halved - 4-5
- Dressing
- Extra virgin olive oil - 1 tbsp.
- Salt - ¼ tsp.
- Orange juice - 2 tbsp.

1. Combine all of the salad ingredients in a large bowl.
2. Dressing ingredients should be combined in a small bowl.
3. To get an even coating, toss the salad mix with the ingredients for the dressing.
4. Put the salad on a serving dish and serve.

Leftover recipe storage: Store in a bowl and cover it with a lid, and place the bowl in the refrigerator.

Leftover recipe reheat/reuse instructions: Take the desired quantity from the bowl and serve.

6.5 Mexican Salad

per serving	941 Cal	45.9g	116g	31.6g	19.3g	3287 mg	347 mg

- Salad
- Mint leaves - ¼ cup
- Avocado, cubed - 1
- Black beans, boiled - 1 cup
- Sweet corn, boiled - 2 cups
- Cherry tomatoes, halved -6-8
- Dressing
- Salt - ¼ tsp.
- Ground cumin - ½ tsp.
- Mustard oil - ½ tsp.
- Maple syrup - 1 tsp.
- Pepper - ⅛ tsp.
- Extra virgin olive oil - 3 tbsp.

1. Combine all of the salad ingredients in a large bowl.
2. Dressing ingredients should be combined in a small bowl.
3. To get an even coating, toss the salad mix with the ingredients for the dressing.
4. Put the salad on a serving dish and serve.

Leftover recipe storage: Store in a bowl and cover it with a lid, and place the bowl in the refrigerator.

Leftover recipe reheat/reuse instructions: Take the desired quantity from the bowl and serve.

6.6 Beet Salad

per serving	569 Cal	53.5g	26.2g	5.4g	4g	1259 mg	317 mg

- Salad
- Medium red onion, sliced - 1
- Parsley leaves - ⅛ cup
- Avocados, cubed - 2
- Lettuce leaves - 2 bunch
- Medium beets, steamed and cubed - 2
- Dressing
- White sesame seeds - 1 tbsp.
- White pepper - ⅛ tsp.
- Extra virgin olive oil - 2 tbsp.
- Salt - ¼ tsp.

1. Combine all of the salad ingredients in a large bowl.
2. Dressing ingredients should be combined in a small bowl.
3. To get an even coating, toss the salad mix with the ingredients for the dressing.
4. Put the salad on a serving dish and serve.

Leftover recipe storage: Store in a bowl and cover it with a lid, and place the bowl in the refrigerator.

Leftover recipe reheat/reuse instructions: Take the desired quantity from the bowl and serve.

- Salad
- Peas, boiled - ¼ cup
- Avocado, sliced - 1
- Broccoli florets, steamed - 1 cup
- Large cucumber, lengthwise sliced - 1
- Baby spinach - 2 cups
- Dressing
- Salt - ¼ tsp.
- Maple syrup - ½ tsp.
- Extra virgin olive oil - 1 tbsp.
- Cinnamon powder - ⅛ tsp.
- Pepper - ⅛ tsp.
- Lime juice - 2 tbsp.

1. Combine all of the salad ingredients in a large bowl.
2. Dressing ingredients should be combined in a small bowl.
3. To get an even coating, toss the salad mix with the ingredients for the dressing.
4. Put the salad on a serving dish and serve.

Leftover recipe storage: Store in a bowl and cover it with a lid, and place the bowl in the refrigerator.

Leftover recipe reheat/reuse instructions: Take the desired quantity from the bowl and serve.

- Salad
- Bananas, sliced - 2
- Green apple, peeled and cubed - 1
- Pomegranate seeds - ¼ cup
- Kiwis, sliced - 2
- Peaches, sliced - 2
- Mint leaves - 2 tbsp.
- Dressing
- Orange juice - 2 tbsp.
- Lemon juice - 2 tbsp.
- Lime juice - 1 tbsp.

1. Combine all of the salad ingredients in a large bowl.
2. Dressing ingredients should be combined in a small bowl.
3. To get an even coating, toss the salad mix with the ingredients for the dressing.
4. Put the salad on a serving dish and serve.

Leftover recipe storage: Store in a bowl and cover it with a lid, and place the bowl in the refrigerator.

Leftover recipe reheat/reuse instructions: Take the desired quantity from the bowl and serve.

6.9 Sunny Salad

- Salad
- Kiwi, sliced - ½ cup
- Blueberries - ½ cup
- Mint leaves - ¼ cup
- Orange, peeled and sliced - ½ cup
- Strawberries, halves - ½ cup
- Dressing
- Salt - ⅛ tsp.
- Lime juice - 2 tbsp.
- Pomegranate juice - 2 tbsp.
- Lemon juice - 2 tbsp.

1. Combine all of the salad ingredients in a large bowl.
2. Dressing ingredients should be combined in a small bowl.
3. To get an even coating, toss the salad mix with the ingredients for the dressing.
4. Put the salad on a serving dish and serve.

Leftover recipe storage: Store in a bowl and cover it with a lid, and place the bowl in the refrigerator.

Leftover recipe reheat/reuse instructions: Take the desired quantity from the bowl and serve.

6.10 Quinoa Fruit Salad

- Salad
- Plum, sliced - ¼ cup
- Mint, chopped - 2 tbsp.
- Peach, sliced - ¼ cup
- Strawberries, halves - ¼ cup
- White grapes - ¼ cup
- Quinoa, cooked - ½ cup
- Dressing
- Grapefruit juice - 2 tbsp.
- Lime juice - 2 tbsp.
- Maple syrup - 2 tbsp.

1. Combine all of the salad ingredients in a large bowl.
2. Dressing ingredients should be combined in a small bowl.
3. To get an even coating, toss the salad mix with the ingredients for the dressing.
4. Put the salad on a serving dish and serve.

Leftover recipe storage: Store in a bowl and cover it with a lid, and place the bowl in the refrigerator.

Leftover recipe reheat/reuse instructions: Take the desired quantity from the bowl and serve.

6.11 Dark Salad

- Salad
- Fig, sliced - 1
- Blackberries - 1 cup
- Black grapes - ¼ cup
- Blueberries - 1 cup
- Purple basil leaves - 1 cup
- Dressing
- Blood fruit juice - 2 tbsp.
- Kosher salt - ⅛ tsp.
- Lime juice - 1 tbsp.
- Maple syrup - 1 tsp.
- Pomegranate juice - 1 tbsp.

1. Combine all of the salad ingredients in a large bowl.
2. Dressing ingredients should be combined in a small bowl.
3. To get an even coating, toss the salad mix with the ingredients for the dressing.
4. Put the salad on a serving dish and serve.

Leftover recipe storage: Store in a bowl and cover it with a lid, and place the bowl in the refrigerator.

Leftover recipe reheat/reuse instructions: Take the desired quantity from the bowl and serve.

6.12 Kalpe Salad

- Salad
- Large red apples, sliced - 2
- Kale leaves - 2 bunch
- Walnuts, chopped - ¼ cup
- Pomegranate seeds - ¼ cup
- Cake crumbles - ½ cup
- Dressing
- Grapefruit juice - 1 tbsp.
- Lemon juice - 3 tbsp.
- Lime juice - 1 tbsp.
- Maple syrup - 1 tsp.
- Salt - ⅛ tsp.

1. Combine all of the salad ingredients in a large bowl.
2. Dressing ingredients should be combined in a small bowl.
3. To get an even coating, toss the salad mix with the ingredients for the dressing.
4. Put the salad on a serving dish and serve.

Leftover recipe storage: Store in a bowl and cover it with a lid, and place the bowl in the refrigerator.

Leftover recipe reheat/reuse instructions: Take the desired quantity from the bowl and serve.

CHAPTER 7

SOUPS

   7.1 Butternut Squash Soup

	108 Cal	9g	6g	4.7g	3g	36 mg	1448 mg
per serving							

- Medium sweet potato, peeled and cubed - 1
- Nutmeg, grated - ⅛ tsp.
- Extra virgin olive oil - ¼ cup
- Ground black pepper - ½ tsp.
- Salt - ½ tsp.
- Large butternut squash, peeled and cubed - 1
- Large onion, chopped - 1
- Ginger, finely grated - 3-inch piece
- Large cloves garlic, smashed - 4
- Vegetable broth - 8 cups
- Pumpkin seeds. For serving - 2 tbsp.
- Cashew cream, for serving - 4 tbsp.

1. On medium heat, warm up a large pot.

2. In the hot pot, add the onions, olive oil, and a pinch of salt. For approximately 3 minutes, while stirring occasionally, cook until the onion is transparent.

3. Garlic, squash, sweet potato, and broth should be combined in a bowl. Bring the pot of water to a boil. After the allotted time is up, add the ginger and mix well. To ensure the squash and sweet potato are cooked through, continue cooking for another 5-10 minutes.

4. For a smooth soup, use a blender for three to five minutes to blend the soup.

5. Depending on your own preference, season with black pepper, salt, and nutmeg.

6. Place a dollop of cashew cream and some pumpkin seeds on top of the soup before serving.

Leftover recipe storage: Store in a bowl and cover it with a lid, and place the bowl in the refrigerator.

Leftover recipe reheat/reuse instructions: Take the desired quantity from the refrigerator, heat in the microwave or on a pan and serve.

- Kosher salt - 1 tsp.
- Onion powder - ½ tsp.
- Vegetable broth - 1 ½ cups
- Almond milk, unsweetened - 1 cup
- Extra virgin olive oil - 1 tbsp.
- Garlic powder - 1 tsp.
- Brussels sprout halves, ocean mist farms season & steam - 16-ounce bag
- Toasted bread pieces - for serving
- Ground black pepper - ¼ tsp.

1. Season and steam a bag of sprouts with salt, pepper, garlic powder, onion powder, and olive oil.
2. Remove the Brussels sprouts from the bag and microwave them for 3 to 7 minutes, or until tender.
3. Blend soup for 1-2 minutes in a blender, purée cooked Brussels sprouts.
4. For a smooth and creamy consistency, blend the broth and milk for one to three minutes on high.
5. Serve soup in bowls, with toasted bread for dipping.

Leftover recipe storage: Store in a bowl and cover it with a lid, and place the bowl in the refrigerator.

Leftover recipe reheat/reuse instructions: Take the desired quantity from the refrigerator, heat in the microwave or on a pan and serve.

 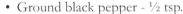

- Ground black pepper - ½ tsp.
- Coconut oil - 1 tbsp.
- Kosher salt - 1 tsp.
- Red curry powder - 1 tsp.
- Yellow onion, chopped - 1
- Garlic, minced - 1 tsp.
- Ginger, grated - 2 tbsp.
- Vegetable broth - 28 ounces
- Carrots, chopped - 3 cups
- Chopped peanuts - for serving
- Dried oregano - for serving
- Grated black pepper - for serving
- Mint leaves - for serving
- Sliced red chilies - for serving

1. Start by melting the coconut oil in a large saucepan over low to medium heat.
2. If you want your onions to be tender, you should cook them for around 5-6 minutes while stirring occasionally.
3. After adding the garlic and garlic, cook for 1 minute.
4. Combine the carrots, red curry powder, and vegetable broth in a bowl and stir well.
5. First, you want to bring the soup to a boil, and then you want to reduce the heat and let it simmer for 30 minutes.
6. In a blender, puree the soup until it reaches a creamy consistency.
7. Garnish cups of the soup with crushed peanuts, red chiles, mint leaves, crushed black pepper, and dried oregano.

Leftover recipe storage: Store in a bowl and cover it with a lid, and place the bowl in the refrigerator.

Leftover recipe reheat/reuse instructions: Take the desired quantity from the refrigerator, heat in the microwave or on a pan and serve.

7.4 Sweet Pea Soup

per serving	117 Cal	0.6g	23.9g	5.8g	5.8g	554 mg	304 mg

- Cauliflower florets - 1 ½ cups
- Broccoli florets - 1 cup
- Large russet potato, washed and cubed - 1
- Small onion, chopped - 1
- Black pepper - 1 tsp.
- Sea salt - 1 tsp.
- Bay leaves - 2
- Baby spinach - 2 cups
- Medium carrots, chopped - 2
- Snap peas - 3 cups
- Garlic, peeled - 5 cloves
- Vegetable stock - 6 cups
- Mint leaves for serving - 2 tbsp.
- Fresh snap peas for serving - 2-3 tbsp.
- Grilled bread - for serving

1. A large soup pot should be placed over high heat and filled with all the soup ingredients except the spinach and salt.
2. When the carrots and potatoes are mushy to the touch, turn the heat down to medium-low, cover, and simmer for another 25 minutes.
3. Put the soup pot on a cooling rack for 20 minutes after you've removed it from the heat.
4. In a blender, blitz the spinach with the salt and the cooled soup until the mixture is silky smooth and creamy.
5. Smooth out the soup with a wand blender.
6. Serve the soup in bowls, topped with fresh snap peas and mint, and accompanied by grilled bread.

Leftover recipe storage: Store in a bowl and cover it with a lid, and place the bowl in the refrigerator.

Leftover recipe reheat/reuse instructions: Take the desired quantity from the refrigerator, heat in the microwave or on a pan and serve.

7.5 Cauliflower Soup

per serving	130 Cal	2.1g	19.4g	11.6g	6.7g	968 mg	1324 mg

- Pepper - ¼ tsp.
- Pink salt - ½ tsp.
- Garlic powder - 1 ½ tsp.
- Onion powder - 1 ½ tsp.
- Bay leaf - 1
- Large head cauliflower, chopped - 1
- Dried thyme - 1 tsp.
- Leeks, chopped - 2
- Nutritional yeast - 2 tbsp.
- Vegetable broth - 6 cups
- Roasted cauliflower floater for serving - 1
- Crushed pepper, for serving - ⅛ tsp.
- Mint leaves, finely chopped for serving - 2 tbsp.

1. To prepare, place all ingredients in a big saucepan and bring to a boil over medium heat, except the serving ingredients.
2. Reduce heat and simmer for 20–25 minutes, or until cauliflower is tender.
3. When the cauliflower is tender, add it to the prepared soup in a blender and purée until silky.
4. Serve with a floater of roasted cauliflower and mint, and sprinkle crushed pepper on top.

Leftover recipe storage: Store in a bowl and cover it with a lid, and place the bowl in the refrigerator.

Leftover recipe reheat/reuse instructions: Take the desired quantity from the refrigerator, heat in the microwave or on a pan and serve.

7.6 Golden Beet Soup

- Fresh sage, chopped - 1 tbsp.
- Ground pepper - ¼ tsp.
- Lemon juice - ½
- Yellow onion, chopped - 1 cup
- Ginger, minced - 1 tbsp.
- Kosher salt - 1 tsp.
- Extra virgin olive oil - 2 tbsp.
- Carrots, chopped - 4 cups
- Vegetable broth - 4 cups
- Golden beets, chopped - 6 cups
- Garlic cloves, chopped - 6
- Black pepper, for serving - ⅛ tsp.
- Cashew cream for serving - 3 tbsp.
- Cilantro - for serving

1. Preheat the oil in a big saucepan over medium heat.
2. Throw all the ingredients (beets, carrots, onion, ginger, sage, garlic, lemon zest, salt, and pepper) into a bowl and stir them around until everything is coated.
3. The garlic, onion, and ginger should be cooked for 10 to 15 minutes over low heat, or until tender and fragrant.
4. bring it to a boil.
5. Cook for 40 to 50 minutes in a medium-low heat.
6. In a blender, puree the soup until it reaches a creamy consistency.
7. Distribute the soup to guests and accompany it with a dollop of sour cream and some chopped cilantro on the side. Before serving, sprinkle some freshly ground black pepper on top.

Leftover recipe storage: Store in a bowl and cover it with a lid, and place the bowl in the refrigerator.

Leftover recipe reheat/reuse instructions: Take the desired quantity from the refrigerator, heat in the microwave or on a pan and serve.

7.7 White Bean and Tomato Soup

- Tomato paste - ¼ cup
- Ground black pepper - ½ tsp.
- Ground cumin - ½ tsp.
- Large onion, chopped - 1
- Cane sugar - 1 tbsp.
- Olive oil - 1 tbsp.
- Smoked paprika - 1 tsp.
- Celery ribs, chopped - 2
- Salt - 2 tsp.
- Canned fire-roasted tomatoes chopped - 27 oz.
- Vegetable stock - 3 cups
- White kidney beans drained and rinsed - 4½ cups
- Garlic chopped - 5 cloves
- Mint leaves - for garnish

1. heat the olive oil in a large saucepan over medium heat.
2. Add onion and celery and cook for approximately 10 minutes, or until the onion and celery are golden brown.
3. Cook for a further two to three minutes, stirring constantly after adding the garlic, smoked paprika, and cumin. Next, add the other soup ingredients and mix well. Cook at a boil for approximately 20 minutes (add little water according to the desired consistency).
4. Put the soup in bowls and sprinkle mint leaves on top.

Leftover recipe storage: Store in a bowl and cover it with a lid, and place the bowl in the refrigerator.

Leftover recipe reheat/reuse instructions: Take the desired quantity from the refrigerator, heat in the microwave or on a pan and serve.

7.8 Corn Soup

| per serving | 208 Cal | 8.1g | 32.6g | 5.7g | 8.9g | 355 mg | 122.5 mg |

- Nutritional yeast - ¼ cup
- Smoked paprika - ½ tsp.
- Coconut milk - 1 14.5 oz. Can
- Bay leaf - 1
- Medium white onion, finely chopped - 1
- Yukon gold potatoes, diced - 1 pound
- Garlic, minced - 2-3 cloves
- Corns - 4 cups
- Broth - 5 cups
- Corn, for serving - 2 tbsp.

1. The onions should be sautéed for three minutes in a big saucepan, or until they have lost their raw flavor and become transparent. After that, add the garlic and cook it for a minute.
2. Next add potatoes, smoked paprika, bay leaf, and broth cook for 5 minutes.
3. You should soften the potatoes and corn in the cooking process. Bay leaf, please remove from soup.
4. Coconut cream and nutritional yeast should be combined in a soup bowl.
5. In a blender, puree the soup until it reaches a creamy consistency.
6. Top the soup with corn and serve it in bowls.

Leftover recipe storage: Store in a bowl and cover it with a lid, and place the bowl in the refrigerator.

Leftover recipe reheat/reuse instructions: Take the desired quantity from the refrigerator, heat in the microwave or on a pan and serve.

7.9 Mushroom Soup

| per serving | 498 Cal | 48g | 16g | 9g | 5g | 880 mg | 802 mg |

- Garlic, finely chopped - 2 cloves
- Coconut milk - 2 tbsp.
- Dried herbs - 1 tsp.
- Mushrooms, sliced - 8 oz.
- Olive oil - 1 tbsp.
- Onion, diced - 1
- Soy sauce - 1 tbsp.
- Vegetable stock powder - 1 tsp.
- Water - 1 cup
- Fried mushroom slices for serving - 3
- Fresh herb - for serving

1. Olive oil should be heated to a medium temperature in a medium saucepan. Incorporate the onions, and heat them down till translucent.
2. Leave them in the oven to bake for a few minutes, or until they release their moisture and shrink to roughly half their original size.
3. Place the onions back in the saucepan and add the garlic and dry herbs, continue cooking for one more minute.
4. Then mix together the soy sauce, coconut milk, water, and stock powder.
5. On low heat, cook for 3 minutes.
6. In a blender, puree the soup until it reaches a creamy consistency.
7. Serve the soup in a bowl with slices of fried mushrooms and herbs on top.

Leftover recipe storage: Store in a bowl and cover it with a lid, and place the bowl in the refrigerator.

Leftover recipe reheat/reuse instructions: Take the desired quantity from the refrigerator, heat in the microwave or on a pan and serve.

- Black pepper - grind to taste
- Can whole peeled tomatoes, including liquid - 1 28-ounce
- Cashew milk - ½ cup
- Drained oil-packed sun-dried tomatoes - 2 tbsp.
- Dried basil - 1 tsp.
- Dried oregano - 1 tsp.
- Garlic, minced - 1 clove
- Medium yellow onion, chopped - 1
- Nutritional yeast flakes - 1 tbsp.
- Organic canola oil - 1 tsp.
- Salt - 1 ½ tsp.
- Tomato paste - 3 tbsp.
- Vegetable bouillon cube - 1
- Water - ½ cup
- Black pepper, for serving - ⅛ tsp.
- Chives for serving - 2 tbsp.

1. Preheat the oil in a big saucepan over medium heat.
2. For about three to four minutes, or until translucent and fragrant, cook the onions and garlic.
3. Cook for 8-10 minutes after adding water, a vegetable bouillon cube, dried oregano, dried basil, ½ tsp. of salt, black pepper, nutritional yeast flakes, tomato paste, and oil-packed sun-dried tomatoes that have been drained.
4. In a blender, puree the soup until it is completely smooth.
5. Put the soup that was blended back into the pot.
6. Cook for 5-10 minutes after adding the milk.
7. Pour the soup into bowls and add chives and black pepper to taste as a garnish.

Leftover recipe storage: Store in a bowl and cover it with a lid, and place the bowl in the refrigerator.

Leftover recipe reheat/reuse instructions: Take the desired quantity from the refrigerator, heat in the microwave or on a pan and serve.

7.11 Pumpkin Apple Soup

- Chopped fresh sage - 2 tbsp.
- Extra virgin olive oil - 2 tbsp.
- Garlic, minced - 3 cloves
- Ground ginger - 2 tsp.
- Large carrot, chopped - 1
- Large granny smith apples, chopped - 3
- Yellow onion, chopped - 1
- Vegetable broth - 4-6 cups
- Red kabocha pumpkin, cubed - 4-pound
- Pumpkin seeds for serving - 2 tbsp.

1. Preheat the oil in a big saucepan over medium heat.

2. Allow the onions, garlic, and ginger to cook for approximately 7 minutes, or until tender.

3. Next add the pumpkin cubes, carrots, apples, and sage and cook for a total of 5 minutes.

4. Slowly simmer the pumpkin, apples, and carrots in the vegetable broth for 30–35 minutes, or until the vegetables are tender.

5. In a blender, puree the soup until it reaches a creamy consistency.

6. Sprinkle pumpkin seeds on top of the soup in bowls.

Leftover recipe storage: Store in a bowl and cover it with a lid, and place the bowl in the refrigerator.

Leftover recipe reheat/reuse instructions: Take the desired quantity from the refrigerator, heat in the microwave or on a pan and serve.

7.12 Lentil Soup

- Coriander powder - ½ tsp.
- Cumin powder - ½ tsp.
- Large carrot, chopped - 1
- Lemon juice - 1
- Onion, chopped - 1
- Paprika powder - 1 ½ tsp.
- Pepper - ¼ tsp.
- Salt - ¼ tsp.
- Crushed tomatoes - 14 oz.
- Celery ribs, chopped - 2
- Dried lentils - 2 cups
- Dried bay leaves - 2
- Garlic cloves, minced - 2
- Olive oil - 2 tbsp.
- Vegetable broth - 6 cups

1. A big saucepan should be placed on the stove and heated to medium heat to prepare the oil. Cook the onion and garlic for 2 minutes in the heated oil.

2. Next add celery, sweet onion and carrots.

3. To get tender celery and carrots and a sweet onion, allow 7–10 minutes of cooking time.

4. Replace the lemon and salt with the other ingredients and stir. Once the water boils, reduce the heat and simmer the lentils for about 35 minutes, or until tender.

5. Bay leaves should be removed from the soup and stored elsewhere.

6. In a blender, puree the soup until it reaches a creamy consistency.

7. Serve the soup in bowls for each person.

Leftover recipe storage: Store in a bowl and cover it with a lid, and place the bowl in the refrigerator.

Leftover recipe reheat/reuse instructions: Take the desired quantity from the refrigerator, heat in the microwave or on a pan and serve.

CHAPTER 8

VEGETARIAN DISHES

8.1 Quesadillas

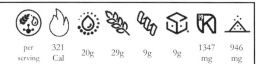

per serving	321 Cal	20g	29g	9g	9g	1347 mg	946 mg

- Filling
- Dried oregano - ½ tsp.
- Cayenne pepper - 1 pinch
- Ground cumin - 1 tsp.
- Red bell pepper, chopped - 1
- Red onion, chopped - ½
- Chili powder - ½ tsp.
- Fine sea salt - ½ tsp.
- Fresh baby spinach - 1-2 cups
- Extra-virgin olive oil - 1 tbsp.
- Black beans, drained and rinsed - 2 8 oz. Can
- Spread
- Lemon juice - 1 ½ tbsp.
- Green chilies, diced - 1 4 oz. Can
- Cashews - 1 cup
- Salt - ¾ tsp.
- Water - 6 tbsp.
- Jarred jalapeno slices - 6-8
- Assembly
- Large flour tortillas - 4
- Salsa - for serving

1. In a big pan, heat the oil over medium heat and add all the filling ingredients.

2. After 8 minutes, check on the onion and bell pepper to see whether they are tender.

3. Sprinkle some water on the sticky area if necessary.

4. Put all the spread ingredients in a high-speed blender and mix until smooth while the veggies are cooking. It's possible to experiment with various flavors and make any necessary modifications. Move it as you finish the filling.

5. Add the black beans, cumin, oregano, chili powder, cayenne pepper, and salt when the onion and peppers have softened. Toss the fresh spinach in the oven for approximately 5 minutes, or until it has lost it's crispness.

6. In a large dish, combine the cooked black bean filling with the other ingredients.

7. In order to gently cover everything in the big pan, spread a tiny bit of olive oil all over everything. (Don't go nuts!) Prepare the tortilla by warming it in a skillet.

8. Spread some sauce over the top of the tortilla. Then, put the black bean filling on only half of the tortilla. Wait 2–4 minutes, or until the bottom of the tortilla starts to get golden.

9. Fold the tortilla in half and cover one half with the black bean filling with a spatula to transfer the quesadilla to a plate. It's best served hot with salsa and triangles.

Leftover recipe storage: Store in the container and cover it with lid, place the container in the refrigerator.

Leftover recipe reheat/reuse instructions: Take the desired quantity from the refrigerator, heat in the microwave or on a pan and serve.

- Dried raw chickpeas, picked over and soaked for at least 4 hours - 1 cup
- Extra-virgin olive oil - ¼ cup + 1 tbsp.
- Fine sea salt - 1 tsp.
- Freshly ground black pepper - ½ tsp.
- Garlic, quartered - 4 cloves
- Ground cinnamon - ¼ tsp.
- Ground cumin - ½ tsp.
- Packed fresh cilantro - ½ cup
- Packed fresh parsley - ½ cup
- Roughly chopped red onion - ½ cup

1. Turn the temperature up to 375 degrees Fahrenheit and position the oven rack in the center.

2. To uniformly cover a big, rimmed baking sheet with olive oil, pour a quarter cup of the oil into the pan and then flip the pan to coat the surface.

3. Soak the chickpeas overnight in water and drain them before combining them with cinnamon, cumin, onion, pepper, salt, garlic, cilantro, parsley, and remaining 1 tbsp. of olive oil in a food processor. Mix the ingredients by pulsing them together. It takes around a minute of processing time to get the mixture completely smooth.

4. Grab a serving size of the mixture equal to roughly 2 tbsp.. Form falafel burgers approximately 2 inches in diameter and half an inch in thickness. Put the falafels on a skillet that has been gently greased.

5. Prepare the falafels for baking and bake for 25-30 minutes, or until golden brown on both sides. When you are halfway through, carefully turn them over. These falafels can stay in the refrigerator for up to 4 days, or they may be frozen for many months.

Leftover recipe storage: Store in box and cover it with lid, place the box in refrigerator/freezer.

Leftover recipe reheat/reuse instructions: Take the desired quantity from the refrigerator, heat in the microwave or on a pan and serve.

- Plant-based milk - 1 cup
- Nutritional yeast - 1 tbsp.
- Onion, diced - ½
- Cornstarch - ½ tbsp.
- Freshly ground nutmeg - ¼ tsp.
- Baby spinach - 4 cups
- Wheat penne pasta - 1 1/3 cup
- Garlic cloves, diced - 2
- Cashews - ½ cup
- Olive oil – as needed
- Pepper - according to taste
- Salt - according to taste

1. Put the cashews in the small dish with the hot wate

2. Cook the pasta according to the package's instruct the pasta cooking water before draining the pasta.

3. Combine the drained cashews, plant-based milk, n any other spices to taste. Make sure there are no cl

4. The next step is to heat some olive oil in a skillet o garlic, cook for 5 minutes, or until the onion is tran

5. For softer spinach and a hotter, somewhat thicker mixture for about 7 minutes. For those who find t the reserved pasta water may be added. Now mix i salt and pepper.

6. Finish by separating the pasta into two bowls, eac and pepper.

Leftover recipe storage: Store in the container and cover it with lid, place the container in the refrigerator.

Leftover recipe reheat/reuse instructions: Take the desired quantity from the refrigerator, heat in the microwave or on a pan and serve.

- Kirby cucumber - 1
- Large clove garlic - 1
- Crustless white bread cubes - ½ cup
- Extra-virgin olive oil - ½ cup + 1 tbsp.
- Coriander seeds, lightly crushed - ½ tsp.
- Cumin seeds - ½ tsp.
- Green bell pepper - 1
- Sugar - ½ tsp.
- Sherry vinegar - 2 tbsp.
- Tomatoes, halved - 3 ¼ pounds
- Freshly ground black pepper - according to taste
- Kosher salt - according to taste

1. Warm up a grill pan over moderate heat. For three minutes, toast the cumin seeds, coriander seeds, and ½ cups of olive oil in a pan over low heat. Liquids should be measured using a special cup. In a small dish, combine 3 tbsp. of the spiced oil with roughly half of the seeds; set aside the remaining seeds for garnish.

2. Put the bread cubes in a bowl and cover them with water. Let them sit there for 2 minutes. Make sure to remove any water by draining and wringing it out.

3. Make a paste by mashing the garlic with the flat side of a knife after you've chopped it and added some salt.

4. The tomatoes may be grilled for 3–5 minutes each side, or until they are blackened, after being mixed with the remaining tbsp. of olive oil in a dish. Combine one-half of the roasted tomatoes with the bread, garlic paste, sugar, vinegar, and a pinch of salt in a blender. Bring together the ingredients and blend until uniform. Pour roughly half of the spiced oil into the measuring cup while the machine is running. Put the contents of the bowl through a fine-mesh sieve. Combine the remaining spiced oil with the tomatoes, bread, garlic paste, sugar, vinegar, and a pinch of salt in a bowl.

5. Allow the soup to cool for at least two hours.

6. The cucumber and pepper should be diced very finely. You may season to taste with salt and pepper. Place the diced veggies and reserved spicy oil in dishes and top with the tomato gazpacho.

Leftover recipe storage: Store in a bowl and cover it with a lid, and place the bowl in the refrigerator.

Leftover recipe reheat/reuse instructions: Take the desired quantity from the refrigerator, heat in the microwave or on a pan and serve.

- Cakes
- Old bay seasoning - 2 tsp.
- Chickpeas, drained and ¼ cup liquid reserved - 2 15-ounce cans
- Honey mustard - 1 tsp.
- Slices white bread, cut into small pieces - 2-3
- Parsley, chopped - 2 tbsp.
- All-purpose flour - 2/3 cup
- Kosher salt - according to taste
- Cream of tartar - 1 pinch
- Lemon juice - 1 tbsp.
- Canola oil - for frying
- Sauce
- Old bay seasoning - 1 pinch
- Dill pickle brine - 1 tbsp.
- Honey mustard - ½ tsp.
- Whole dill pickle, finely chopped - ½
- Vegan mayonnaise - ¼ cup
- Lemon wedges - for serving

1. Fill a large mixing bowl halfway with chickpea liquid for the chickpea cakes. The cream of tartar should be whipped in until the mixture is thick and frothy.

2. Put the bread cubes in a bowl and coat them with a mixture of parsley, lemon juice, Old Bay seasoning, mustard, and bread. Give it five to seven minutes, or until the bread is pliable, for the bread to rest.

3. To pass the time, slice the chickpeas very thinly. When the bread and vegetable combination is done, add the chickpeas and toss to incorporate. Form into eight patties, each ¾ inch thick, with smooth edges. Put the patties in the fridge for at least an hour, covered.

4. Tartar sauce can easily made by combining mayonnaise, honey mustard, Old Bay, pickle, and pickle brine in a small dish. Refrigerate until ready to serve.

5. To preheat the oven, choose the "bake" setting and enter 350 F. Spread the flour out on a platter and season it well with salt. In a big, nonstick pan, heat the oil over medium heat. You should use flour to dust half of the cakes.

6. Fry the cakes for three minutes on each side in heated oil, or until they get a golden crispness. To prevent them from browning too soon, adjust the temperature as necessary. Placing all the cakes on a baking sheet after you've done the same with the rest is a good idea. Bake for 5 minutes, or until heated all the way through, then sprinkle with salt. Serve the crab cakes made with chickpeas with wedges of lemon and tartar sauce.

Leftover recipe storage: Store in box and cover it with lid, place the box in refrigerator/freezer.

Leftover recipe reheat/reuse instructions: Take the desired quantity from the refrigerator, heat in the microwave or on a pan and serve.

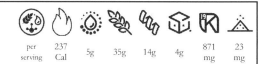

- Lentils
- Medium tomatoes, diced - 2
- Onion, diced - 1
- Serrano chili, sliced in ½-inch optional - 1
- Water - 2 cups
- Garlic, thinly sliced - 4 cloves
- Ginger, peeled and minced - 1 ½ -inch piece
- Tempering oil
- Canola oil - 1 tbsp.
- Black mustard seeds - ½ tsp.
- Chopped fresh cilantro leaves - handful
- Red lentils - 1 cup
- Cumin seeds - ½ tsp.
- Generous turmeric powder - ½ tsp.
- Paprika - ½ tsp.

1. To clean the lentils, just place them in a strainer and run water through them. Put them in a dish, cover them with water, and let them sit for 30 minutes. Rinse and stow.

2. In a medium saucepan, combine the lentils, onions, garlic, ginger, tomatoes, chile (if using), and 2 cups of water. In a pot, bring to a boil over medium heat. Remove any film or scum that may have formed. (avoid adding salt, however) Lentils take longer to cook when salted, but the extra time is well worth it. Reduce to medium-low heat, cover, and simmer for 30 to 40 minutes, or until the lentils are very soft, almost transparent, and coming apart.

3. Lentils include starch that is released when they are combined, thus mashing some of them creates a thicker consistency. You may season to taste with salt and pepper.

4. To season the oil, combine the ground cumin and mustard seeds in a small dish. The spice powders should be combined in a separate bowl.

5. 1 tbsp. of canola oil should be heated over medium heat in a small to medium sized pan. After the oil has reached a shimmer, add the seeds and immediately cover the pan so you don't be blasted with oil and seeds as they pop. Toss the spices together. This is referred to as "blooming," and it is what you want. Watch out for overheating. There shouldn't be more than a 30-second bloom time for the combination.

6. Slowly add the oil mixture to the lentils, keeping a close watch on the pot in case it begins to boil over. Combine all the ingredients by mixing them together. Spread the red lentils out on a plate and sprinkle the cilantro on top.

Leftover recipe storage: Store in the container and cover it with lid, place the container in the refrigerator.

Leftover recipe reheat/reuse instructions: Take the desired quantity from the refrigerator, heat in the microwave or on a pan and serve.

- Ground black pepper - ¼ tsp.
- Brown sugar - ¼ cup
- Ketchup - ½ cup
- Uncooked mushroom cut into strips - ½ pound
- Medium onion, diced - 1
- Worcestershire sauce - 1 tbsp.
- Dry navy beans, soaked overnight - 2 cups
- Salt - 2 tsp.
- Dry mustard - ¼ tsp.
- Molasses - 3 tbsp.

1. In a pot, bring the navy beans and the water in which they were soaked to a boil.

2. Cook the beans for about 1-2 hours on low heat. Place it aside to drain.

3. Preheat the oven to 325° Fahrenheit.

4. Put half of the beans in the bottom of a casserole dish that's at least 2 quarts in size. On top of the beans, sprinkle half the mushroom slices and half the onions. It's time to rebuild the layers.

5. Combine the ketchup, molasses, brown sugar, Worcestershire sauce, salt, pepper, and dry mustard in a large saucepan over medium heat. Get the water boiling.

6. Sauce should be poured over the beans. Cover the pot with a lid or aluminum foil and pour in enough water to submerge the beans.

7. Put it in an already-on oven for 12 hours to cook. Keep the beans from drying out by checking on them every half an hour or so for the next 1.5 to 2.5 hours of cooking time.

Leftover recipe storage: Store in the container and cover it with lid, place the container in the refrigerator.

Leftover recipe reheat/reuse instructions: Take the desired quantity from the refrigerator, heat in the microwave or on a pan and serve.

- Freshly ground black pepper - according to taste
- Bay leaf - 1
- Jalapeño, minced - 1
- Black beans, drained and rinsed - 3 (15-oz.) Cans
- Chili powder - 1 tsp.
- Chopped fresh cilantro - for garnish
- Extra-virgin olive oil - 2 tbsp.
- Garlic, minced - 2 cloves
- Ground cumin - ½ tsp.
- Kosher salt – according to taste
- Low-sodium chicken or vegetable broth, plus more as needed - 3 cups
- Medium red onion, finely chopped - 1
- Tomato paste - 1 tbsp.
- Lime wedges - for serving (optional)

1. Olive oil should be heated over medium heat in a large pot. To get a tender and translucent onion, cook it for 5 minutes in the heated oil. Add garlic and jalapeños and cook for about 2 minutes, or until the garlic and jalapeños start to release their pleasant aroma. Once you've added the tomato paste and stirred it to coat the veggies, cook them for an additional minute. Coat everything with the salt, pepper, cumin, and chili powder by mixing them together.

2. Toss in the can of black beans and some chicken stock. After include the bay leaf, bring the soup to a boil. Reduce the heat and simmer for 15 to 20 minutes, until it has thickened and reduced in size.

3. Remove the bay leaf and let it cool before putting it back into the soup. As soon as the soup has been blended, serve it.

Leftover recipe storage: Store in a bowl and cover it with a lid, and place the bowl in the refrigerator.

Leftover recipe reheat/reuse instructions: Take the desired quantity from the refrigerator, heat in the microwave or on a pan and serve.

- Panko (Japanese breadcrumbs) - ¼ cup
- Freshly ground black pepper - ¼ tsp.
- Cooked brown rice, at room temperature - ½ cup
- Garlic, chopped - 1 clove
- Italian-style tomato sauce, divided - 1 cup
- Shallot, chopped - 1
- Small eggplant, unpeeled and chopped - 1
- Whole-wheat flour - 1 tbsp.
- Fine sea salt, divided - 1 tsp.
- Whole-wheat hoagie rolls, split and toasted - 2 (6-inch)
- Olive oil, divided - 3 tbsp.
- Fresh cremini mushrooms, sliced - 6 ounces
- Fresh basil, torn - for serving

1. Over medium heat, place 2 tbsp. of oil, ¼ tsp. of salt, and the eggplant in a large nonstick pan. Stirring often, cook the eggplant for 5 minutes to get a golden brown color and a softer texture. Toss the mushrooms with the shallot and garlic and cook for 4–5 minutes, or until the mushrooms are browned. Tend to the meatball mixture in the food processor for at least 5 minutes to cool. Use a cloth to wipe off the pot.

2. Combine the rice, panko, flour, pepper, and the remaining ¾ tsp. of salt in a food processor and pulse until combined. After around 15 pulses, the ingredients should have combined. (It'll be sticky in the end.) Form eight balls of dough (about the size of golf balls).

3. In a large, nonstick skillet, heat the remaining tbsp. of oil over medium heat. After 10–12 minutes, add the mushroom meatballs and cook, rotating occasionally, until browned. The stove should be turned off.

4. Put a rack in the oven that's 8 inches from the broiler and turn it on. Arrange the toasted buns on a baking sheet with a rim. Half a cup of tomato sauce spread equally across the rolls' interiors Add the remaining meatballs and tomato sauce. You should broil the subs for about two minutes, or until they reach the desired temperature. You may top your meal with the torn basil if you want.

Leftover recipe storage: Store in an airtight container and cover it with lid, place the container in refrigerator.

Leftover recipe reheat/reuse instructions: Take the desired quantity from the refrigerator, heat in the microwave or on a pan and serve.

- Heavy whipping cream, divided - ¼ cup 2 tsp.
- Chopped celery - ½ cup
- White Grape Juice - ¾ cup
- Frozen sweet peas - 1 cup
- Chopped leek (pale green and white area only) - 1 cup
- Dried porcini mushrooms - 1 ounce
- Black pepper, divided - 1 tsp.
- Fresh mushrooms - 1 ½ pound
- Kosher salt, divided - 1 ¾ tsp.
- Medium carrots, lengthwise halved and sliced - 2
- Mixed fresh woody herbs, chopped - 2 tbsp.
- Water - 2 ½ cups
- Olive oil - 3 tbsp.
- Unsalted butter - 3 tbsp.
- All-purpose flour - 3 ½ tbsp.
- Packages frozen puff pastry (1 sheet), thawed - 5 (17.3-ounce)

1. Put the rack in the top third of the oven.

2. Turn it on to 425 degrees Fahrenheit in the oven. In a small saucepan, bring the water and mushrooms to a boil over high heat. Turn off the stove and let the boiling mushrooms cool for 30 to 35 minutes with the lid off.

3. Meanwhile, on a large rimmed baking sheet, toss together the fresh mushrooms, oil, and ½ tsp. each of salt and pepper. Separate the mushrooms out fairly. Cook for 25 minutes, stirring every 15 minutes, until the mushrooms are tender and gently browned. Get it out of the oven! Turn the oven down to 375 degrees Fahrenheit.

4. In a cast-iron skillet of about 10 inches in diameter, melt the butter over low heat. To soften the carrots, cook for approximately 2 minutes while stirring often. Leeks, celery, and ½ tsp. of salt should be combined in a bowl. Maintain a steady stirring for approximately 2 minutes, or until the leek is tender. For approximately 30 seconds, or until the herbs begin to release a pleasant aroma, stir them often. After adding the flour, cook for 1-2 minutes, stirring constantly. To avoid burning the flour, scrape the bottom of the pan as you add the white grape juice. Continue cooking for 1 minute while stirring constantly. Employing a slotted spoon, transfer the porcini mushrooms to the pan. Add the porcini water gradually, being careful to leave any sediment at the bottom of the pan. Add the cream, about a quarter cup. In a pot, bring to a boil over medium heat. Cook for about 4 minutes, while stirring often, bring to a boil to thicken the sauce. The stove should be turned off. Add the baked mushrooms and peas, and season with salt and pepper to suit. Place the dish on a big, deep baking sheet with a rim.

5. Roll out the puff pastry into a 12-inch square on a lightly floured board. Just lop off approximately ½ inches from each corner and you'll have a rough circle. The dough is flattened using a rolling pin. Quickly unroll the dough over the filling in the pan. Trim the overhanging dough and tuck and crimp the edges into the dish. Use kitchen shears to slash four 1-inch-long vents into the pastry's surface. Finally, using a pastry brush, apply the remaining 2 tbsp. of cream on the dough.

6. Position the rack in the upper third of the oven and place the baking sheet and pan inside. Bake for 15 minutes at 375 degrees Fahrenheit, or until the crust is lightly browned. The pastry should be baked for 30 to 35 minutes, or until it is golden, fluffy, and crisp. Hold off on serving it for at least 5 minutes so it can cool down.

Leftover recipe storage: Store in the container and cover it with lid, place the container in the refrigerator.

Leftover recipe reheat/reuse instructions: Take the desired quantity from the refrigerator, heat in the microwave or on a pan and serve.

CHAPTER 9

VEGAN DISHES

6 | 15" | 22"

9.1 Mushroom Wrap

| per serving | 164 Cal | 4g | 26.1g | 8.1g | 8.1g | 247 mg | 216 mg |

- Filling
- Chat masala - 1 tsp.
- Finely chopped garlic - 1 tbsp.
- Finely chopped peeled fresh ginger - 1 tbsp.
- Fresh lemon juice - 2 tsp.
- Garam masala - 2 tsp.
- Ground turmeric - ½ tsp.
- Kosher salt - 1 tsp.
- Medium-size red bell pepper, sliced - 1
- Medium-size red onion, sliced - 1
- Plain whole-milk yogurt - ¾ cup
- Tofu - 8 oz.
- Salad
- Black pepper - ¼ tsp.
- Dark brown sugar - 1 tsp.
- Fresh lime juice - 2 tbsp.
- Kosher salt - ½ tsp.
- Very thinly sliced green cabbage - 1 cup
- Very thinly sliced red onion - 1 cup
- Whole-wheat flour tortillas - 6 (6-inch)

1. In a medium bowl, whisk together the yogurt, garlic, ginger, garam masala, lemon juice, chat masala, and turmeric. Scoop out and save ¼ cups of the yogurt marinade in a second, smaller bowl. Put the remainder of the marinade ingredients into a medium bowl and stir to combine. Coat the onion and bell pepper and add them to the pan. Combine the paneer with a quarter cup of the marinade in a separate small bowl and stir well. The recommended chill time for each bowl is between 30 minutes and 8 hours in the fridge.

2. Adjust the oven rack so that it is 6 inches from the heating element and preheat the oven to 500 degrees Fahrenheit. In a single layer, scatter the marinated veggies onto a rimmed baking sheet coated with aluminum foil. Stirring occasionally, bake for 12 minutes. Take it out of the oven. Place a broiler pan on the middle rack of the oven. On a baking sheet, combine the marinated veggies and tofu. Cook the tofu in the broiler for 6-8 minutes, or until it is no longer raw in the center and the veggies are crisp-tender. In a medium bowl, combine all of the ingredients before seasoning with the salt. The best way to keep anything warm is to cover it and put it away. Reduce the heat in the oven to 200 degrees Fahrenheit.

3. Don't just throw the onion in there without washing it and drying it off first. In a medium bowl, toss together the onion, cabbage, lime juice, jiggery, salt, and pepper. Putting aside.

4. Tortillas should be prepared in accordance with the package's instructions. To keep the tortillas warm, place them on a baking sheet and heat it in the oven.

5. Take a tortilla and eat it. Place an 8-inch square of aluminum foil on the table. Prepare a paratha by placing half of it on the foil and the other half on the counter. Spread tortillas with 1 tbsp. of the spicier mango-mint chutney. Wrap the tortillas around the cabbage salad and filling mixture, using the cabbage salad as a base. Mix in a pinch of chat masala. Roll the tortillas like a burrito, folding the bottom up and the sides in toward the center, and then holding it in place with foil. Repeat with the remaining tortillas, chutney, cabbage salad, filling, and chat masala.

Leftover recipe storage: Store in the container and cover it with lid, place the container in the refrigerator.

Leftover recipe reheat/reuse instructions: Take the desired quantity from the refrigerator, heat in the microwave or on a pan and serve.

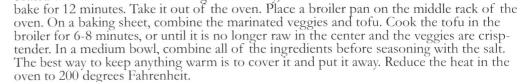
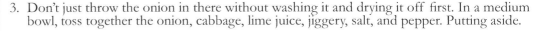

- Pickles
- Distilled white vinegar - 1 cup
- Medium daikon, cut lengthwise 2-inch - 1
- Kosher salt, divided - 2 tsp.
- Granulated sugar, divided - 3 tbsp.
- Resh medium, sliced -
- Kimbap rice
- Uncooked tamanishiki rice - 1 cup
- Sesame oil - 1 tbsp.
- Kosher salt - 1 tsp.
- Kosher salt - 1 tsp.
- Rice vinegar - 2 tsp.
- Shoots
- Extra-virgin olive oil - 1 tbsp.
- Pea shoots - 3 cups
- Additional
- Small avocado, halved and cut lengthwise - 1
- Nori sheets - 6 (8x7 ½ -inch)
- Scallions, trimmed and cut lengthwise - 8
- Extra-virgin olive oil - for drizzling and for serving
- Flaky sea salt, to taste - for serving
- Sauce - for serving

1. Combine the jalapeños with ½ tbsp. of sugar and 1 tsp. of kosher salt in a medium bowl and stir to combine. Daikon, the remaining ½ tbsp. of sugar, and the remaining tsp. of kosher salt should be combined in a medium bowl that won't react with the sugar or salt. Allow 30 minutes for the bowls to come to room temperature. Each bowl requires ½ cup white vinegar. Refrigerate until ready to use, up to a week.

2. In a sieve, wash the rice and dry it off by shaking it. In accordance with the package's instructions, prepare the rice. In a large bowl, combine the rice. In a bowl, combine the rice vinegar, kosher salt, and sesame oil. After that, pour the liquid over the rice and stir it in with a rice paddle or wooden spoon. Wrap a plastic bag around the bowl containing the rice.

3. In a large cast-iron pan, melt the butter over medium heat. Combine the pea shoots, oil, and salt in a large mixing dish. Cook, tossing occasionally, for 1 to 2 minutes, or until the pea shoots are mostly wilted and have a light char. In a medium bowl, cool the pea shoots for 10 minutes.

4. Wrap a sushi mat in plastic wrap and lay it horizontally on a work surface. Place one sheet of nori on the mat, short end facing you. Spread ¾ cup rice evenly across the nori, leaving 1 ½ inch of the top short end uncovered. (To keep the rice from sticking to your hands, soak them in water or daikon pickling liquid.) Cut the second sheet of nori in half lengthwise and place one half on the rice's bottom half.

5. Arrange Place 3 pickled daikon sticks, 3 avocado slices, 8 scallion pieces, approximately 8 pickled jalapeno slices, and ¼ cup pea shoots horizontally along the nori's short bottom side Arrange the ingredients so that they protrude about 1 inch from the nori's sides. Tightly roll it up.

6. Sprinkle flaky sea salt over the kimbap and drizzle olive oil over the roll pieces. Divide the roll into 10 equal pieces. Serve with your preferred sauce.

Leftover recipe storage: Store in the container and cover it with lid, place the container in the refrigerator.

Leftover recipe reheat/reuse instructions: Take the desired quantity from the refrigerator, heat in the microwave or on a pan and serve.

9.3 Butter Squash Steak

per serving	474 Cal	19.3g	80.7g	7.2g	15.2g	2420 mg	189 mg

- Large butternut squash, one with a long thick neck - 1
- Extra-virgin olive oil - 1 tbsp.
- Unsalted butter, cut into pieces - 2 tbsp.
- Sage leaves - 6
- Garlic cloves, crushed - 2
- Fresh lemon juice - 1 tbsp.
- Kosher salt, - according to taste
- Freshly ground pepper – according to taste

1. Save the squash's neck and base for another use. Peel after removing the stem. The neck is supported by a base that has been split in half lengthwise to form two lobes. Remove the round side on the outside of each piece to make two ¾ inch thick steaks (about 6 oz. each). Keep the cut-off sides for another project.

2. Preheat the oil on a big grill on the stovetop. After approximately 15 minutes, or when both sides are thoroughly browned and the squash steaks are readily sliced with a fork, you may zigzag-turn them. Steak, oil, butter, sage, and garlic should all be combined in the same pan. To make the butter pool on one side, tilt the pan in your direction and continue basting the steaks with butter with a large spoon. Cook for about a minute, basting occasionally, or until the butter stops bubbling, smells nutty, and begins to brown. Put the nuts and butter in a bowl and add the lemon juice when you've taken them from the heat. You may season to taste with salt and pepper.

3. Place the squash steaks on a plate and top with the sauce.

Leftover recipe storage: Store in the container and cover it with lid, place the container in the refrigerator.

Leftover recipe reheat/reuse instructions: Take the desired quantity from the refrigerator, heat in the microwave or on a pan and serve.

9.4 Crispy Tofu with Glaze

per serving	361 Cal	31g	14.4g	8.2g	10.5g	195 mg	892 mg

- Unseasoned rice vinegar - 3 tbsp.
- Pure maple syrup - 3 tbsp.
- Canola oil - ½ cup
- Crushed red pepper flakes - ½ tsp.
- Low-sodium soy sauce - ¼ cup
- Ginger, very thinly sliced – 1 ½ piece
- Block firm tofu - 1 (12-oz.)

1. Drain the tofu and put it between layers of paper towels to soak up any extra liquid. Create nine cubes.

2. Combine the ginger, red pepper flakes, red wine vinegar, maple syrup, and soy sauce in a bowl and stir.

3. Heat the canola oil in a nonstick skillet over medium heat. Carefully add the tofu when bubbles appear on the surface of the oil. To get a crisp and dark brown bottom, cook for 3 to 5 minutes while stirring occasionally. Carefully reverse direction and repeat on the other side. When transferring the oil to a bowl, use a slotted spoon or spatula to hold back the tofu. Soak up the soy sauce in the water and pour it into the pan. For 4 minutes, or when the glaze is thick enough to coat a spoon, reduce the heat to medium and baste the tofu occasionally.

4. Serve the tofu on a serving platter or bowl.

Leftover recipe storage: Store in the container and cover it with lid, place the container in the refrigerator.

Leftover recipe reheat/reuse instructions: Take the desired quantity from the refrigerator, heat in the microwave or on a pan and serve.

9.5 Curried Black-Eyed Peas

| per serving | 254 Cal | 18.9g | 19.2g | 6.5g | 2.6g | 425 mg | 908 mg |

- Small yellow onions, diced - 2
- Salt, plus more as needed - 1 tbsp.
- Unsweetened coconut milk - 1 (13.5-ounce) can
- Cilantro, chopped - 1 bunch
- Habanero, stemmed, seeded, and super-small dice - 1
- Black pepper - 1 tsp.
- Olive oil - 1/4 cup
- Water - 2 cups
- Dried black-eyed peas (soaked overnight) - 3 cups
- Curry powder - 3 tbsp.
- Garlic cloves, thinly sliced - 6
- Limes juice - 2

1. For 5 to 8 minutes over medium heat cook, garlic, onion, habanero, olive oil, and a dash of salt in a big saucepan.

2. Keep cooking until the onions have completely soaked up the curry powder. Next, add the water and beans. Turn reduce the heat to medium-low and cook covered for 20 minutes.

3. Reduce the heat to low, add the coconut milk, and simmer the beans for 30 minutes, or until soft.

4. In a bowl, combine the pepper, cilantro, and lime juice. Then, toss in a tbsp. of salt. Just try it! You can add more salt to the beans if you want, and you can keep them on low heat until they are seasoned and cooked the way you like.

Leftover recipe storage: Store in the container and cover it with lid, place the container in the refrigerator.

Leftover recipe reheat/reuse instructions: Take the desired quantity from the refrigerator, heat in the microwave or on a pan and serve.

9.6 Yogurt Lentil Curry With Spinach

| per serving | 354 Cal | 14g | 41.7g | 17.5g | 6.9g | 802 mg | 684 mg |

- Onions, finely chopped - 2
- Yellow lentils - 100g
- Ground turmeric - ½ tsp.
- Salt - ½ tsp.
- Chili powder - ½ tsp.
- Fresh root ginger, peeled and chopped - 1-inch
- Ghee - 2 tbsp.
- Plain yogurt - 3 tbsp.
- Boiling water - 400ml
- Fresh spinach leaves - 7 oz.

1. To a pot of boiling water, salt, turmeric, and ginger, along with the yellow lentils, add the indicated quantity. Get the water boiling. Ten to twelve minutes covered on low to medium heat. After adding the spinach, continue cooking for another 5 minutes, or until the spinach has wilted and the lentils are mushy.

2. Meanwhile, use a pan over low to medium heat to melt the ghee. Put in the onions, and simmer for 10 to 12 minutes, or until they become golden. When done, stir in the chili powder. Putting aside.

3. To make a puree, purée the cooked lentils in a blender, food processor, or with a hand blender. Finally, fold the yogurt into the sauce. The dal should be served in a dish with the fried onions on top.

Leftover recipe storage: Store in the container and cover it with lid, place the container in the refrigerator.

Leftover recipe reheat/reuse instructions: Take the desired quantity from the refrigerator, heat in the microwave or on a pan and serve.

- Salt - ¾ tsp.
- All-purpose flour, plus more - 1 cup
- Instant mashed potato flakes - 1 cup
- Flaxseeds soaked in water - 5 tbsp.
- Butter, melted - 3 tbsp.
- Black pepper - for garnish
- Chopped parsley - for garnish

1. In a medium bowl, combine 1 cup of instant mashed potato flakes with butter. Combine with a cup of hot water and a thorough mixing. In a large bowl, combine one big egg, ¾ tsp. of salt, and all-purpose flour. Briefly knead the ingredients together until smooth.

2. In a big saucepan, bring approximately 4 inches of salted water to a simmering boil. Three tbsp. of fat (butter or EVOO) and two to two and a half tbsp. of dough (formed to a thickness of ¾ inch) are required. Cut it into pieces that are ¾ inches wide and long. Roll each piece while pressing it against the fork prongs. As a result, the gnocchi will curl slightly, with one side flat and the other ridged. Cook for 2 minutes, or until the gnocchi float in the simmering water. When you bite into them, they should be chewy and stay together. If they are too soft or crumbly, knead in up to 3 tbsp. all-purpose flour and a small amount of flaxseed mixture.

3. Try the test again. When the dough is done rising, cut it into three or four 14-inch-thick ropes. Cut the ropes into pieces that are ¾ inches long, shape the dough as described above with a fork, and place the pieces on a lightly floured baking sheet. Get the water to a low boil again. Let the water boil, but don't let it boil all the way. Cook the gnocchi, uncovered, until it floats, which should about a third to half of the way be through. Mix the gnocchi together in a big bowl.

4. Serve the gnocchi in bowls topped with whatever you want.

Leftover recipe storage: Store in the container and cover it with lid, place the container in the refrigerator.

Leftover recipe reheat/reuse instructions: Take the desired quantity from the refrigerator, heat in the microwave or on a pan and serve.

- Medium zucchinis, cut into ½ -inch dice - 4
- Extra-virgin olive oil - 1 tbsp.
- Freshly ground black pepper - according to taste
- Kosher salt - ½ tsp.

1. Combine the collard greens, peanuts, miso, and garlic in a food processor. You'll end up with a paste that has some noticeable chunks. In a running food processor, gently add the olive oil via the feed tube. To get the desired consistency, extra oil may be used. You may adjust the seasoning with salt, pepper, and more lemon juice. Putting aside.

2. Preheat the oven to 450 degrees Fahrenheit.

3. Prepare a parchment paper-lined baking sheet.

4. Spread the zucchini in a single layer on a baking sheet after mixing it with olive oil and salt. Bake for 18–20 minutes, or until zucchini begins to color. Before serving, season the zucchini with pepper.

Leftover recipe storage: Store in the container and cover it with lid, place the container in the refrigerator.

Leftover recipe reheat/reuse instructions: Take the desired quantity from the refrigerator, heat in the microwave or on a pan and serve.

- Ground turmeric - ½ tsp.
- Paprika - ½ tsp.
- Garlic clove, finely chopped - 1
- Small onion, finely chopped - 1
- Virgin coconut oil - 1 tbsp.
- coconut milk, Unsweetened - 1 ¼ cup
- Kosher salt, plus more - 1 ¼ tsp.
- Raw cashews, soaked overnight - 2 cups
- Curry powder - 2 tsp. Ginger, peeled, finely chopped - 1 ½ inch piece

1. After the cashews have been drained and washed, set them aside.

2. Coconut oil should be melted in a big, heavy saucepan over low to medium heat. Add onion and cook; when the onion is translucent and transparent, add the ginger and garlic and continue cooking for another 5 to 7 minutes, stirring occasionally.

3. In a large bowl, combine the curry powder, turmeric, paprika, and ¼ tsp. of salt. Stir to combine and coat the aromatics. Allow the aromatics to cook for 2 minutes, or until they have developed a pleasant scent and are lightly browned.

4. Add half a cup of water and use a wooden spoon to scrape the bottom of the pan to remove any browned pieces. Add the coconut milk and the cashews that you set aside and bring to a boil. To make cashews somewhat softer and liquid reduced by two-thirds, cook for 25–35 minutes, stirring regularly and adjusting heat as required. If desired, add a splash of lime juice and serve.

Leftover recipe storage: Store in the container and cover it with lid, place the container in the refrigerator.

Leftover recipe reheat/reuse instructions: Take the desired quantity from the refrigerator, heat in the microwave or on a pan and serve.

- Large onion, finely chopped - 1
- Chopped golden or brown raisins - 1/3 cup
- Extra-virgin olive oil - ¼ cup
- Finely chopped mixed tender herbs - 1 cup
- Flaxseeds mix with water for 10 minutes - 2 tbsp.
- Fresh lemon juice - 1 tbsp.
- Kosher salt - according to taste
- Large savoy or green cabbage leaves (from 1 large head) - 12–14
- Long-grain white rice, rinsed - ¾ cup
- Pine nuts - ½ cup
- Freshly ground black pepper - according to taste
- Sumac, plus more for serving - 2 tbsp.
- Unsalted butter - 3 tbsp.

1. Spread clean paper towels in a number of layers on a baking pan. To make the cabbage leaves tender and brilliant green, boil them in a saucepan of salted water for approximately 2 minutes at a time. To chill the leaves, we use a dish of cold water. To cook the rice, keep the water in the pot. Prepare a baking sheet and set it out for draining the cabbage leaves.

2. In a pot of rapidly boiling water, cook the rice for 3 to 6 minutes, stirring often, or until the grains have expanded and risen to the top (depending on the quality of rice). Sample some rice to determine whether it's cooked to the perfect al dente texture (rice will finish cooking when baked inside the cabbage). Rice may be stopped from cooking by quickly rinsing it under cold water. Again, rinse under cold water and transfer to a very large mixing bowl.

3. Sweep out the cooking vessel. A quarter cup of oil should be heated in a saucepan over medium heat. Keep an eye on it and stir it around every so often for 7 to 9 minutes, or until the onion is tender and yellow. Cook for another 5 minutes, stirring often, until the onion is practically jammy and the pine nuts have darkened in color and have a toasted aroma. Combine the herbs, raisins, and 2 tbsp. of sumac in a bowl and stir to combine. For around two to three minutes, while stirring often, the herbs should soften in color and provide a pleasant aroma. Remove from fire, add lemon juice, and let stand, covered, for 5 minutes to cool.

4. Combine the onion-rice mixture well. You may season to taste with salt and pepper. Simply place three heaping tbsp. of filling in the leaf's center and fold the notch side of the leaf up and over the filling to enclose it. As though making a burrito, the leaf is folded in half and wrapped up.

5. A single layer of cabbage rolls, seam side down, should be placed in the pot. Over medium heat, melt the butter and bring the water to a simmer in a 12-cup measuring cup. For 18–25 minutes over low heat, with the cover on, steam the rolls until the filling is cooked through and the leaves are soft.

6. Serve the cabbage rolls on a serving platter.

Leftover recipe storage: Store in the container and cover it with lid, place the container in the refrigerator.

Leftover recipe reheat/reuse instructions: Take the desired quantity from the refrigerator, heat in the microwave or on a pan and serve.

CHAPTER 10

FISH AND SHELLFISH

10.1 Cedar Planked Salmon

per serving	678.4 Cal	45.8g	6 1/3g	10.6g	0.4g	1144.3 mg	981.2 mg

- Canola oil - 1/3 cup
- Chopped green onions - ¼ cup
- Grated fresh ginger - 1 tbsp.
- Minced garlic - 1 tsp.
- Rice vinegar - 1 ½ tbsp.
- Salmon fillets, skin removed - 2 (2 pound)
- Sesame oil - 1 tsp.
- Soy sauce - 1/3 cup
- Untreated cedar planks - 3 (½ inch)

1. edar boards need to be soaked in hot water for at least an hour. If you can spare the time, soak for at least ten minutes longer.

2. A sauce made of soy sauce, canola oil, rice vinegar, sesame oil, green onions, ginger, and garlic should be served in a shallow dish.

3. Toss the salmon fillets around in the soy sauce until they are well coated. Marinate in the fridge for 15 minutes minimum, and up to an hour.

4. Turn the grill to medium heat. Arrange the boards on the grill. Heating the boards to the point where they smoke and crackle is ideal.

5. After marinating, remove the fish and place it on the planks. You may discard the marinade.

6. Take the lid off the grill. Cook the salmon on a grill for approximately 20 minutes, or until it flakes easily when poked with a fork. When you remove the salmon off the grill, it will continue to cook for a few minutes.

Leftover recipe storage: Store in the container and cover it with lid, place the container in the refrigerator.

Leftover recipe reheat/reuse instructions: Take the desired quantity from the refrigerator, heat in the microwave or on a pan and serve.

10.2 Grilled Marinated Shrimp

| per serving | 447.1 Cal | 37.5g | 3.7g | 25.3g | 0.4g | 308.4 mg | 800 mg |

- Ground black pepper - 1 tsp.
- Dried oregano - 2 tsp.
- Garlic, minced - 3 cloves
- Skewers - 6
- Hot pepper sauce - 2 tbsp.
- Lemon, juiced - 1
- Olive oil - 1 cup
- Salt - 1 tsp.
- Tomato paste - 1 tbsp.
- Large shrimp, peeled and deveined with tails attached - 2 pounds
- Chopped fresh parsley - ¼ cup

1. Create a sauce by combining olive oil, parsley, lemon juice, hot pepper sauce, garlic, tomato paste, oregano, salt, and black pepper. Keep a little bit to use as a basting sauce. Place the shrimp in a big, sealable plastic bag along with the remaining marinade. Marinate for two hours in the fridge, covered.

2. Turn the grill on to medium-low heat. Stick the skewers through the shrimp three times near the tail and one time near the head. Take away the sauce.

3. Apply oil to the grill rack to prevent sticking. In a skillet over medium heat, cook the shrimp for approximately 5 minutes on each side, basting often with the reserved marinade.

Leftover recipe storage: Store in the container and cover it with lid, place the container in the refrigerator.

Leftover recipe reheat/reuse instructions: Take the desired quantity from the refrigerator, heat in the microwave or on a pan and serve.

10.3 Scott Ure's Clams

| per serving | 191.5 Cal | 12.8g | 4.3g | 3.9g | 1g | 187.3 mg | 63.5 mg |

- Garlic, minced - 6 cloves
- Chopped fresh parsley - ½ cup
- Extra virgin olive oil - 2 tbsp.
- Broth - 1 cup
- Butter - 2 tbsp.
- Small clams in shell, scrubbed - 50

1. Clams need to be washed to get rid of any sand or dirt.

2. Preheat the oil in a big saucepan over medium heat. 1 minute in hot oil, sauté garlic until tender. Start the broth boiling. Cook until half of the broth has been used up.

3. Cover the pot and steam the clams until they begin to open. Cook until most or all of the clams open, then add the butter and cover the pot. Any clams that do not open should be discarded.

4. Divide the clams and broth between two large bowls. Serve with chopped parsley on top.

Leftover recipe storage: Store in the container and cover it with lid, place the container in the refrigerator.

Leftover recipe reheat/reuse instructions: Take the desired quantity from the refrigerator, heat in the microwave or on a pan and serve.

10.4 Grilled Alaska Salmon

per serving	307.2 Cal	21.5g	4.6g	23.3g	3.1g	613.2 mg	649.3 mg

- Salt - ½ tsp.
- Fillets salmon - 8 (4 ounce)
- Sesame oil - 1 tsp.
- Crushed red pepper flakes - 2 tsp.
- Ground ginger - 1 ½ tsp.
- Garlic, minced - 2 cloves
- Brown sugar - 3 tsp.
- Green onions, chopped - 4 tbsp.
- Balsamic vinegar - 4 tbsp.
- Soy sauce - 4 tbsp.
- Peanut oil - ½ cup

1. In a medium, nonporous glass dish, place half of the salmon fillets. Peanut oil, soy sauce, vinegar, green onions, brown sugar, garlic, ginger, red pepper flakes, sesame oil, and salt should all be combined in a separate medium bowl. Toss together and serve over the fish. Marinate the salmon for four to six hours in the fridge, covered.

2. Prepare a grill by brushing it lightly with oil and positioning the coals at a distance of approximately five inches from the grate.

3. Fish fillets should be grilled until they flake easily when tested with a fork, about 10 minutes per inch of thickness. Flip the fish over at the halfway point of cooking.

4. Serve with your favorite sauce.

Leftover recipe storage: Store in the container and cover it with lid, place the container in the refrigerator.

Leftover recipe reheat/reuse instructions: Take the desired quantity from the refrigerator, heat in the microwave or on a pan and serve.

10.5 Salmon Patties

per serving	224.4 Cal	10.4g	9g	22.3g	1.1g	290.8 mg	522.8 mg

- Canned salmon - 1 (14.75 ounce) can
- Egg - 1
- Chopped onion - ¼ cup
- Seasoned dry bread crumbs - ½ cup
- Olive oil - 1 tbsp

1. Drain and set aside the salmon liquid. Combine the egg, onion, bread crumbs, and salmon in a mixing bowl.

2. Form into little cakes or patties. Add the salmon's saved juices if the mixture is too dry to shape into patties.

3. Heat the olive oil in a skillet. Grill the patties in a pan. Both sides are brown, and it's simple to flip them. Prepare food in a paper towel-lined drain and serve hot.

Leftover recipe storage: Store in the container and cover it with lid, place the container in the refrigerator.

Leftover recipe reheat/reuse instructions: Take the desired quantity from the refrigerator, heat in the microwave or on a pan and serve.

10.6 Garlic-Lemon Scallops

| per serving | 408 Cal | 24.4g | 8.9g | 38.5g | 0.2g | 635.4 mg | 987.9 mg |

- Butter - ¾ cup
- Minced garlic - 3 tbsp.
- Large sea scallops - 2 pounds
- Salt - 1 tsp.
- Pepper - ⅛ tsp.
- Fresh lemon juice - 2 tbsp.

1. Butter has to be melted in a big pan over medium heat. Just when the garlic takes on a pleasant aroma, cook it for a few seconds. Make sure the fish is firm and clear by frying it for a few minutes on one side and then switching it over.

2. Put the scallops on a serving tray and make the sauce by combining the butter, salt, pepper, and lemon juice. After the scallops have been cooked, pour the sauce over them.

Leftover recipe storage: Store in the container and cover it with lid, place the container in the refrigerator.

Leftover recipe reheat/reuse instructions: Take the desired quantity from the refrigerator, heat in the microwave or on a pan and serve.

10.7 Steamed Mussels

| per serving | 484.5 Cal | 24.4g | 21.4g | 48.3g | 2.7g | 236 mg | 1472.5 mg |

- Thai red curry paste - 1 ½ tbsp.
- Chopped fresh cilantro - 2 cups
- White sugar - 1 tbsp.
- Asian fish sauce - 1 tbsp.
- Fresh mussels, scrubbed and debearded - 5 pounds
- Fresh lime juice - 1/3 cup
- Unsweetened coconut milk - 1 (13.5 ounce) can
- Minced garlic - 1 ½ tbsp.
- White grape juice - 1/3 cup

1. Combine the lime juice, coconut milk, grape juice, curry paste, garlic, fish sauce, and sugar in a large stockpot and stir to combine. To dissolve the sugar and curry paste, bring to a boil over high heat while stirring constantly. Before adding mussels, let the water boil for at least 2 minutes. When the mussels have opened, which should take around 5 to 8 minutes, uncover and stir occasionally.

2. Take the mussels off the heat and throw away any that haven't opened. Mix the mussels and their liquid with the cilantro in a dish to serve.

Leftover recipe storage: Store in the container and cover it with lid, place the container in the refrigerator.

Leftover recipe reheat/reuse instructions: Take the desired quantity from the refrigerator, heat in the microwave or on a pan and serve.

10.8 Crab Cakes

per serving	216.1 Cal	15.2g	5.7g	13.9g	0.8g	256.4 mg	354.4 mg

- Lemon juice - 4 tsp.
- Egg - 1
- Minced green onions - 1 tbsp.
- Dried tarragon - 1 tsp.
- Red pepper flakes - ⅛ tsp.
- Mayonnaise - 3 tbsp.
- Crabmeat - 8 ounces
- Crushed buttery round crackers - ½ cup
- Butter - 1 tbsp.

1. Mix the egg, mayonnaise, green onions, lemon juice, tarragon, and pepper flakes in a medium bowl. Carefully mix in the crabmeat without breaking it up. Add the cracker crumbs slowly, adding more as needed to get the right texture. Use the crab mixture to make four patties.

2. Butter should be melted in a pan over medium heat.

3. Cook the patties for about 5-6 minutes each side in a pan, or until they reach a golden brown color.

Leftover recipe storage: Store in the container and cover it with lid, place the container in the refrigerator.

Leftover recipe reheat/reuse instructions: Take the desired quantity from the refrigerator, heat in the microwave or on a pan and serve.

10.9 Broiled Scallops

per serving	272.9 Cal	9.4g	6.8g	38.3g	0.2g	755.1 mg	2232.2 mg

- Bay scallops - 1 ½ pounds
- Melted butter, or as needed - 2 tbsp.
- Lemon juice - 2 tbsp.
- Garlic salt - 1 tbsp.

1. Preheat the broiler on high.

2. After washing the scallops, put them in a shallow baking dish. 2 tbsp. of melted butter, lemon juice, and garlic salt, to taste

3. When the broiler is hot, broil the scallops for 6 to 8 minutes, or until they begin to turn golden.

4. Take them out of the oven and serve them with extra melted butter on the side so people can dip them.

Leftover recipe storage: Store in the container and cover it with lid, place the container in the refrigerator.

Leftover recipe reheat/reuse instructions: Take the desired quantity from the refrigerator, heat in the microwave or on a pan and serve.

- Evaporated milk - 2 (12 ounce) cans
- Water - 4 cups
- Butter - 1 cup
- Salt - according to taste
- Ground black pepper - according to taste
- Oysters, drained - 2 (8 ounce) cans

1. In a large saucepan, combine the evaporated milk and water and simmer on low. Slowly bring to a boil.

2. The butter should be combined with the liquid. Black pepper and salt are optional. Stirring occasionally, bring to a simmer, and cook for 5–7 minutes, or until the butter has melted.

3. To cook oysters, just combine them with the liquid and simmer for 15 minutes, or until the shells curl, then serve.

Leftover recipe storage: Store in a bowl and cover it with a lid, and place the bowl in the refrigerator.

Leftover recipe reheat/reuse instructions: Take the desired quantity from the refrigerator, heat in the microwave or on a pan and serve.

- Paprika - ½ tsp.
- Canola oil cooking spray
- Plain dry breadcrumbs - ½ cup
- Whole-grain cereal flakes - 1 cup
- Lemon pepper - 1 tsp.
- Garlic powder - ½ tsp.
- Salt - ¼ tsp.
- All-purpose flour - ½ cup
- Large egg whites, beaten - 2
- Tilapia fillets, cut into strips - 1 pound

1. Preheat the oven to 450 degrees Fahrenheit. Prepare a baking sheet by spraying it with cooking spray and placing a wire rack inside.

2. Use a blender or food processor to chop up the bread into small pieces, then add the cereal flakes, salt, garlic powder, paprika, and lemon pepper. Location: a wide, shallow basin.

3. Prepare a third small bowl for the egg whites, and a second small bowl for the flour. Flour, egg, and the breadcrumb mixture should be used to coat each fish strip. Location: on the rack that has previously been prepared. The fish should be sprayed on both sides with cooking spray before being fried.

4. Wait until the fish flakes easily and the breading is golden brown and crunchy, about 10 minutes in the oven.

Leftover recipe storage: Store in the container and cover it with lid, place the container in the refrigerator.

Leftover recipe reheat/reuse instructions: Take the desired quantity from the refrigerator, heat in the microwave or on a pan and serve.

- White fish, cod or other lean, cut into 12 equal pieces - 18 ounces
- Salt - ¼ tsp.
- Black pepper, ground - ¼ tsp.
- Sesame seeds - ½ cup
- Lemon rind, grated - 2 tsp.
- Parsley, chopped - 1 tbsp.
- Olive oil - 1 tbsp.
- Cooking spray
- Tzatziki sauce, optional - ½ cup
- Skewers - either metal or bamboo

1. Set the grill to a temperature between medium-high and high.
2. Thread three fish pieces onto each skewer.
3. Add a lot of salt and pepper to the fish.
4. Stir together the sesame seeds, parsley, and lemon peel in a large bowl.
5. Use oil to coat the fish.
6. Coat the fish skewers in the seed mixture evenly.
7. The fish should be sprayed with cooking oil.
8. Grill the fish for approximately 2-3 minutes each stick side, or until the seeds are brown and the fish is firm.
9. Serve with your favorite sauce.

Leftover recipe storage: Store in the container and cover it with lid, place the container in the refrigerator.

Leftover recipe reheat/reuse instructions: Take the desired quantity from the refrigerator, heat in the microwave or on a pan and serve.

- Large shrimp, peeled and deveined - 1 pound
- Unsalted butter - 3 tbsp.
- Garlic, minced - 3 cloves
- Kosher salt - ¼ tsp.
- Extra virgin olive oil – as needed
- Cilantro, for garnish - 1 tbsp.
- Skewers - either metal or bamboo

1. Preheat the grill to high heat on the side that does not have any coals.
2. Put a stick through the middle of each shrimp.
3. Salt and pepper the shrimp after you've brushed them with olive oil.
4. Combine the butter and garlic in a separate bowl.
5. The skewers should be cooked on the grill for about 2 minutes on each side.
6. Take the shrimp off the grill and paint them with the garlic and butter mixture right away.
7. Serve with the sauce you like best and some fresh cilantro.

Leftover recipe storage: Store in the container and cover it with lid, place the container in the refrigerator.

Leftover recipe reheat/reuse instructions: Take the desired quantity from the refrigerator, heat in the microwave or on a pan and serve.

10.14 Teriyaki Tuna Skewers

| per serving | 336 Cal | 9g | 4g | 68g | 19.1g | 1070 mg | 1960 mg |

- Fresh tuna steak, cut into 1-inch pieces - 2 pounds
- Teriyaki sauce - 15 ounces
- Sesame oil - 3 ounces
- Ginger, freshly minced - 1 tbsp.
- Garlic, freshly minced - 1 tsp.
- Lemon juice - 1
- Brown sugar - 1 tbsp.
- Sesame seeds, toasted, for garnish - 1 tbsp.
- Skewers - either metal or bamboo

1. Combine the first seven items in a large dish and set aside. Let it sit for 30 minutes.
2. Get the grill going on medium-high heat.
3. Put a stick through the tuna.
4. Grill each side of the skewers for 3–4 minutes, turning them often.
5. Take the tuna off the grill and sprinkle it with sesame seeds.

Leftover recipe storage: Store in the container and cover it with lid, place the container in the refrigerator.

Leftover recipe reheat/reuse instructions: Take the desired quantity from the refrigerator, heat in the microwave or on a pan and serve.

10.15 Tuna Kebabs with Herb Lemon, And Grains

| per serving | 451 Cal | 9.8g | 44.2g | 43.4g | 7g | 762 mg | 626 mg |

- Onion springs, finely chopped, optional - 6
- Tuna steak, cut into 2 inch pieces - 1 pound
- Rose or regular harissa - 2 tbsp.
- Large lemons, juiced - 2
- Cumin, toasted and crushed, optional - 1 tsp.
- Medium cucumber, diced, optional - ½
- Mint, chopped, optional - small handful
- Flat-leaf parsley, chopped, optional - small handful
- Yoghurt, optional - 8 tbsp.
- Toasted mixed grains, for serving, optional - 2 ½ cup
- Skewers, either metal or bamboo – 4

1. In a large bowl, combine the tuna, harissa, and 1 tbsp. of lemon juice. Please take a 10-minute break.
2. Blend 1 lemon's juice with the grains, cumin, spring onions, and a big bowl.
3. Prepare a medium-high fire in the grill.
4. Cook the tuna skewers on the grill for two to three minutes each side.
5. Serve the tuna with grains and yogurt after grilling it.

Leftover recipe storage: Store in the container and cover it with lid, place the container in the refrigerator.

Leftover recipe reheat/reuse instructions: Take the desired quantity from the refrigerator, heat in the microwave or on a pan and serve.

CHAPTER 11
SIDES AND SMALL PLATES

11.1 Cuban sandwich Sticks

per serving	151 Cal	6.8g	17.5g	5g	1g	20 mg	345 mg

- Garlic bread slices - 6
- Lettuce leaves - 6
- Deli ham slices - 6
- Cheddar cheese slices, cut from between - 3
- Green olives, pitted - 6
- Skewer, either metal or bamboo - 6

1. On a piece of bread, layer lettuce, cheese, ham, and olives.
2. In the same way, prepare the remaining 5 pieces.
3. Thread the skewer from the top to the bottom of the sandwich.
4. Serve with ketchup and mayonnaise on the side.

Leftover recipe storage: Store in the container and cover it with lid, place the container in the refrigerator.

Leftover recipe reheat/reuse instructions: Take the desire quantity from the refrigerator, heat in microwave and serve.

11.2 Shrimp Skewers

per serving	206 Cal	10g	0g	23g	0.4g	52 mg	1317 mg

- Large shrimp, peeled and deveined - 1 pound
- Olive oil - ½ cup
- Lemon juice - 2 tbsp.
- Salt - ¾ tsp.
- Black pepper - ¼ tsp
- Italian seasonings - 1 tsp.
- Garlic, minced - 2 tsp.
- Parsley, chopped - 1 tbsp.

1. Sealable plastic bag with shrimp, lemon juice, olive oil, salt, black pepper, Italian spice, and garlic.
2. To coat evenly, close the bag and toss.
3. Allow 15 minutes to 2 hours for it to sit. (If the shrimp are marinated for longer than 2 hours, the acid in the lemon will begin to cook them.)
4. Serve with the shrimp threaded onto skewers.
5. Lightly oil the grill grates and set the temperature to medium-high.
6. Grill the shrimp for 2 to 3 minutes each side, or until the flesh is opaque and pink.
7. Serve with lemon wedges and garnished with parsley.

Leftover recipe storage: Store in the container and cover it with lid, place the container in the refrigerator.

Leftover recipe reheat/reuse instructions: Take the desired quantity from the refrigerator, heat in the microwave or on a pan and serve.

11.3 Sesame Tuna Bites

per serving	161 Cal	12g	4g	10.25 g	1.4g	338 mg	287 mg

- Honey - ½ tbsp.
- Avocado, medium - ½
- Soy sauce - ⅛ cup
- Sesame oil - 1 tbsp.
- Lemon juice - ½ tbsp.
- Ginger, freshly minced - ½ tsp.
- Sesame seeds, black and white - ¼ cup
- Olive oil, light - 1 tbsp.
- Fresh tuna, sushi-grade, cut into 1-inch pieces - ½ pound
- Skewers - 6
- Toothpicks - for serving

1. In a big mixing bowl, mix together the tuna, soy sauce, both oils, lemon juice, honey, ginger, and sesame seeds.
2. Marinade for approximately 20 minutes.
3. On a plate, scatter sesame seeds.
4. Roll the tuna in sesame seeds on both sides.
5. Thread the tuna chunks onto a skewer.
6. Grill each side for about 15-20 minutes. (The center should be pink and rare.)
7. Remove from the grill and thread the tuna and avocado onto a toothpick.
8. Serve with your preferred sauce or dip.

Leftover recipe storage: Store in the container and cover it with lid, place the container in the refrigerator.

Leftover recipe reheat/reuse instructions: Take the desire quantity from the refrigerator, and serve.

11.4 Brat Skewers

per serving	137 Cal	9g	17g	9.33g	7.4g	72 mg	377 mg

- Uncooked bratwurst links, cut into 2-inch slices - 16 ounces
- Slices of loaf bread, cut into 2 pieces each - 3
- Low fat cheddar cheese, shredded - ½ cup
- Brown sugar - 3 tbsp.
- Salt, or to taste - 1 tsp.
- Cayenne pepper - ¼ tsp.
- Skewers, either metal or bamboo - 6

1. Mix the bratwurst, sugar, salt, and pepper together in a large mixing bowl.
2. Toss everything together and set aside for 1 hour.
3. Thread the bratwurst onto the skewer.
4. Grill the bratwurst for 15-20 minutes, or until bratwurst is no longer pink, turning frequently.
5. Take the skewers out of the bratwurst.
6. Thread the bread and bratwurst onto the skewer first.
7. Crumble the shredded cheese over the bread and bratwurst.
8. Grill for a minute or two until toasty and serve immediately.

Leftover recipe storage: Store in the container and cover it with lid, place the container in the refrigerator.

Leftover recipe reheat/reuse instructions: Take the desired quantity from the refrigerator, heat in the microwave or on a pan and serve.

- Watermelon wedges - 6
- Salt, or to taste - 1 tsp.
- Low fat feta cheese, crumbled - 1 cup
- Mint leaves - 6
- Pop sticks - 6

1. Fill each watermelon wedge with popsicle sticks.
2. Season the watermelon wedges with salt.
3. Serve the watermelon wedges with feta cheese and mint leaves.

Leftover recipe storage: Store in the container and cover it with lid, place the container in the refrigerator.

Leftover recipe reheat/reuse instructions: Take the desire quantity from the refrigerator, and serve.

- Hummus
- Sea salt - ½ tsp.
- Reserved chickpea water - ¾ cup
- Lemon zest - 1 tsp.
- Lemon juice - 1/3 cup
- Cans chickpeas, skinless and drained with water reserved - 2 15 oz.
- Garlic cloves, peeled - 2
- Tahini - 2/3 cup
- Olive oil - 3 tbsp.
- Toppings
- Olive oil - 1 tbsp.
- Paprika - ⅛ tsp.
- Flat-leaf parsley, chopped - 2 tbsp.

1. Mix the hummus ingredients together by pulsing a food processor on low speed.
2. Increase the speed of the food processor gradually and blend for 5 minutes on high, or until hummus is smooth and creamy.
3. Put some paprika and parsley in a bowl, then pour some olive oil over the top.
4. Serve with warm pita bread.

Leftover recipe storage: Store in the container and cover it with lid, place the container in the refrigerator.

Leftover recipe reheat/reuse instructions: Take the desire quantity from the refrigerator, and serve.

11.7 Green Ranch Dip

| per serving | 91 Cal | 8g | 3.6g | 2.8g | 0g | 72.6 mg | 156.7 mg |

- Fresh dill, chopped - ¼ cup
- Tahini - ½ cup
- Water - ½ cup
- Salt - ½ tsp.
- Garlic - 1 clove
- Baby spinach - 1 cup
- Apple cider vinegar - 2 tbsp.

1. In a food processor, combine spinach, tahini, water, dill, vinegar, garlic, and salt until smooth, then serve.

Leftover recipe storage: Store in the container and cover it with lid, place the container in the refrigerator.

Leftover recipe reheat/reuse instructions: Take the desire quantity from the refrigerator, and serve.

---

8 | 5" | 30"

11.8 French Onion Dip

| per serving | 94 Cal | 7.4g | 5.5g | 2.7g | 0.9g | 8.46 mg | 155.5 mg |

- Olive oil - 1 tbsp.
- Medium yellow onion, chopped - 1
- Vegan sour cream - 1 ¼ cups
- Onion powder - ½ tsp.
- Water - 6 tbsp.
- Mineral salt- ¼ tsp.
- Vegan Worcestershire sauce - 1 tsp.
- Garlic powder - ½ tsp.
- Chopped parsley for serving - 2 tbsp.

1. On medium heat, heat the oil in a skillet that doesn't stick. Stir the food constantly for about 10 to 15 minutes.

2. Let 2 tbsp. of water sizzle and evaporate before adding the other 4 tbsp. of water and cooking on low for 25 to 30 minutes, or until the onions are brownie caramelized and smell good.

3. Mix vegan sour cream, garlic powder, onion powder, Worcestershire sauce, and caramelized onions together in a medium bowl.

4. Put the dip in a dish and garnish with parsley before serving.

Leftover recipe storage: Store in the container and cover it with lid, place the container in the refrigerator.

Leftover recipe reheat/reuse instructions: Take the desire quantity from the refrigerator, and serve.

11.9 Pesto

- Extra virgin olive oil - ¼ cup
- Kosher salt - ½ tsp.
- Lemon zest grated - ½ tsp.
- Fresh basil leaves - 1 ½ cups
- Almonds, smoked - 1/3 cup
- Chilled green tea, unsweetened - ¼ cup
- Shelled pistachios, roasted - 1/3 cup
- Large cloves garlic - 2

1. Add basil, almonds, pistachios, tea, garlic, salt, and lemon zest to a food processor; cover, process for 1 minute, and pulse a few times.

2. Pour the oil in while pulsing the food processor until the mixture looks like coarse pesto.

3. Add a pinch of salt to taste.

Leftover recipe storage: Store in the container and cover it with lid, place the container in the refrigerator.

Leftover recipe reheat/reuse instructions: Take the desire quantity from the refrigerator, and serve.

11.10 Avocado Chocolate Dip

- Maple syrup - 1/3 cup
- Salt - ⅛ tsp.
- Large ripe avocados, pitted and peeled - 2
- Almond milk - 2 tbsp.
- Vanilla extract - ½ tbsp.
- Cocoa powder, unsweetened - 2/3 cup

1. In a food processor, combine avocado, maple syrup, cocoa powder, vanilla extract, and salt; process until the dip is smooth, using a spatula to clean off the sides of the food processor as needed.

2. Process the almond milk for another 20-30 seconds in the food processor.

3. Put the avocado chocolate dip in a serving bowl and serve with cookies, bread, or fruits.

Leftover recipe storage: Store in the container and cover it with lid, place the container in the refrigerator.

Leftover recipe reheat/reuse instructions: Take the desire quantity from the refrigerator, and serve.

CHAPTER 12
POULTRY RECIPES

   12.1 Baked Chicken Breasts

per serving	551.8 Cal	26.9g	2.3g	71.6g	0.5g	635.9 mg	834.4 mg

- Salt - ½ tsp.
- Garlic powder - 1 tsp.
- Ground mustard - ½ tsp.
- Parsley flakes - ½ tsp.
- Ground black pepper - ½ tsp.
- Bone-in skinless chicken breasts - 2 (12 ounce)
- Olive oil - 1 tbsp.
- Smoked paprika - 1 tsp.
- Butter - 2 tbsp.
- Parchment paper

1. Turn on the oven to 400 degrees F.
2. In a small mixing bowl, combine together garlic powder, paprika, mustard, parsley, salt, and pepper. Rub olive oil on all sides of each chicken breast, then coat with the spice rub. Put them on a baking sheet. 1 tbsp. butter on top of each breast Cover each breast with parchment paper, tucking it underneath to form a sealed pouch.
3. Bake for another five minutes, or until the juices run clear, and then remove from the oven. A thermometer taken from the middle should show an internal temperature of at least 165 degrees Fahrenheit. Take the chicken out of the oven and let it sit for five minutes.

Leftover recipe storage: Store in the container and cover it with lid, place the container in the refrigerator.

Leftover recipe reheat/reuse instructions: Take the desired quantity from the refrigerator, heat in the microwave or on a pan and serve.

   12.2 Chicken Casserole

per serving	329.8 Cal	7.6g	30.5g	33.6g	4.6g	260.5 mg	902.3 mg

- Ground black pepper - according to taste
- Frozen mixed vegetables - 1 ½ cups
- Reduced-fat cream of chicken soup - 1 (10.75 ounce) can
- Cubed cooked chicken breast - 2 cups
- Low-fat greek yogurt - 1 cup
- Shredded fat-free cheddar cheese - ½ cup
- Avocado oil cooking spray - 1 serving
- Salt – according to taste
- Reduced-fat buttery round crackers crushed – 24

1. The oven has to be preheated to 375 degrees F. Spray a square baking dish, about 8 inches in diameter, with nonstick spray.
2. Cream of chicken soup, chicken, veggies, yogurt, salt, and pepper should all be combined in a large mixing bowl. Sprinkle the Cheddar cheese on top of the dish before baking. Sprinkle smashed crackers and spray avocado oil over cheese.
3. Prepare in an oven at 350 degrees for 30 minutes to ensure heat. Broil for another two to three minutes, or until the crackers are a golden brown, after another spritz with avocado oil.

Leftover recipe storage: Store in the container and cover it with lid, place the container in the refrigerator.

Leftover recipe reheat/reuse instructions: Take the desired quantity from the refrigerator, heat in the microwave or on a pan and serve.

- Bone-in chicken breast halves, skinless - 3
- Chicken broth - 1 (14.5 ounce) can
- Potatoes - 3
- Yellow onion - 1
- Stalks celery - 3
- Canola oil - 2 tbsp.
- All-purpose flour - 2 tbsp.
- Frozen mixed vegetables - 2 cups
- Salt – according to taste
- Pepper - according to taste
- Garlic powder - ¼ tsp.
- Frozen prepared pie crust, thawed - 1 (9 inch)

1. Once the chicken breasts have been washed, they should be placed in a saucepan with enough water to cover them by an inch or so. Sprinkle over some garlic powder, salt, and pepper. Once it begins to boil, turn off the heat and cover it. Leave the saucepan aside to cool.

2. Prepare a 350F oven.

3. Prepare the potatoes as directed (wash, peel, and chop into small cubes) and boil until almost fork-tender. After draining, put away.

4. Prepare the celery by washing and chopping it into manageable bits. You should cut the onion up so that it's easy to eat.

5. Over medium heat, cook the celery and onion in 2 tbsp. of oil in a big, heavy pan for 5 to 8 minutes. The frozen veggies should be cooked for a further 5 minutes. After incorporating the flour, continue cooking for a further 30 seconds.

6. Start boiling the chicken broth. Once it has thickened, toss in the potatoes.

7. Toss the chicken into a food processor and pulse until it's a fine crumb size. Put in as much salt and pepper as you want.

8. Put the filling into a 9-inch deep dish pie plate and top with the pie crust. Crimp the pie crust's edges to the dish to prevent liquids from bubbling over while baking.

9. Bake for 45 minutes at 350 °F, or until the crust is golden then serve.

Leftover recipe storage: Store in the container and cover it with lid, place the container in the refrigerator.

Leftover recipe reheat/reuse instructions: Take the desired quantity from the refrigerator, heat in the microwave or on a pan and serve.

- Ground black pepper – according to taste
- Skin-on, bone-in chicken thighs - 6
- Salt – according to taste
- Garlic powder - 1 pinch

1. Set the temperature to 475 degrees Fahrenheit. A wire rack should be placed in a broiler or baking dish.

2. Chicken thighs should be dried thoroughly using paper towels. Raise the skin carefully and season it with a pinch each of salt, pepper, and garlic powder. It's important to get new skin. Add salt, pepper, and garlic powder to the skin and the underside of the thighs. Hold on the rack.

3. Put in a hot oven for 20 minutes to get a nice golden color. Take the temperature down to 400 degrees Fahrenheit in the oven. If you want clear juices, roast for another 30 minutes. The minimum waiting time before serving is 5 minutes.

Leftover recipe storage: Store in the container and cover it with lid, place the container in the refrigerator.

Leftover recipe reheat/reuse instructions: Take the desired quantity from the refrigerator, heat in the microwave or on a pan and serve.

- Skinless, boneless chicken tenders, cut into ½ -inch strips lengthwise - 4
- Ground black pepper - 1 tsp.
- Kosher salt - 1 tsp.
- Ground paprika - 1 tsp.
- Onion powder - 1 tsp.
- Garlic powder - 2 tsp.
- Panko bread crumbs - 1 ¼ cups
- Large egg, beaten - 1
- Cooking spray

1. To bake well, the oven has to be preheated to 450 degrees F. Prepare an aluminum foil-lined baking sheet by spraying it with cooking spray.

2. The egg should be placed in a wide, shallow bowl. Combine the panko, garlic powder, onion powder, paprika, salt, and pepper in a large zip-top freezer bag.

3. Coating 2 chicken strips with panko breadcrumbs, egg, and shaking Prepare a baking sheet and then transfer the breaded chicken to it. Use the leftover chicken to make a second serving.

4. Every chicken tender needs two coats of cooking spray.

5. Put the tenders in an oven that has been preheated for 7 minutes. 7 minutes extra of baking time should be spent on the other side to ensure that the centers are no longer pink. Take it out of the oven.

6. Turn on the broiler and place a rack in the oven approximately 6 inches from the element.

7. For a crispier finish, broil the tenders for an additional minute or two in a hot oven.

8. Serve with fries and sauce, dip or ketchup.

Leftover recipe storage: Store in the container and cover it with lid, place the container in the refrigerator.

Leftover recipe reheat/reuse instructions: Take the desired quantity from the refrigerator, heat in the microwave or on a pan and serve.

- Whole chickens - 2
- Sugar - 1 cup
- Salt - 1 cup
- Water - 1-gallon
- Apple cider vinegar - 2 cups
- Brown sugar - ¼ cup
- White pepper - 1 tsp.
- Water - 2 cups
- Barbecue sauce - for serving

1. Combine together the chickens, salt, sugar, and a gallon of plain water in a large stockpot. Let it to rest for at least 4-5 hours, preferably overnight (refrigerate sitting it overnight).

2. Truss your chickens, then firmly thread the rotisserie onto the chicken and spit over the grill.

3. Douse the chickens with the mixture of apple cider vinegar, white pepper, brown sugar, and water in a squirt bottle.

4. Cook the chickens for 4-8 hours. Rotate the spit every 20-30 minutes and baste the chickens with the brown sugar mixture every hour.

5. The chicken is done when the thickest part registers 165°F.

6. Serve the chickens immediately with barbeque sauce.

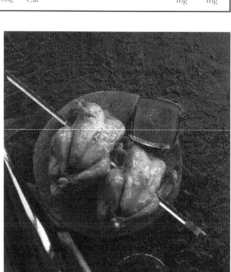

Leftover recipe storage: Store in the container and cover it with lid, place the container in the refrigerator.

Leftover recipe reheat/reuse instructions: Take the desired quantity from the refrigerator, heat in the microwave or on a pan and serve.

- Ground cumin - 1 tsp.
- Garlic cloves, minced - 3
- Red pepper flakes, crushed - ½ tsp.
- Smoked paprika - 1 tsp.
- Brown sugar - 2 tbsp.
- Extra virgin olive oil - 2 tbsp.
- Soy sauce - 2 tbsp.
- Lime juice, fresh - 2 tbsp.
- Chicken thighs, skinless and boneless - 3 pounds
- Fresh ginger, minced - 2 tbsp.
- Skewers - either metal or bamboo
- Chili powder - 1 tsp.
- Peanuts - for serving, optional

1. Trim the chicken of any superfluous fat before cutting it into 1-inch cubes.

2. Put everything but the chicken into a big bowl and stir well.

3. Leave alone for half an hour. Half of the marinade should be set aside for later, and the chicken should be tossed in the remaining marinade to coat.

4. Lightly oil the grill grates and set the temperature to medium-high.

5. The chicken chunks should be threaded onto the skewers.

6. Brush oil onto the grill grates.

7. The chicken skewers need to be grilled for 13-15 minutes, rotating once or twice, until they are cooked through and golden.

8. Put in another two or three minutes of cooking time after brushing with the leftover marinade.

9. Take the skewered chicken off of the grill and let it rest under foil for 5 minutes.

10. Serve with the peanuts on top.

Leftover recipe storage: Store in the container and cover it with lid, place the container in the refrigerator.

Leftover recipe reheat/reuse instructions: Take the desired quantity from the refrigerator, heat in the microwave or on a pan and serve.

- Bell peppers, medium, cut into thick pieces - 6
- Onion, large, cut into thick pieces - 1
- Chili powder - ⅛ cup
- Paprika - ½ tbsp.
- Ground thyme - ¼ tsp.
- Salt - 1 tsp.
- Garlic powder - 1 tsp.
- Black pepper - ¼ tsp.
- Cumin powder - ½ tsp.
- Chicken breasts, boneless - 2
- Cayenne pepper - ⅛ tsp.
- Brown sugar - ½ tbsp.
- Olive oil - 1 tbsp.
- Skewers, either metal or bamboo - 4-6

1. Bell peppers, onion, chili powder, paprika, thyme, garlic, cumin, cayenne pepper, sugar, oil, salt, and black pepper should all be combined in a large mixing bowl.
2. Toss the chicken in the spice mixture to properly coat it. Ten minutes of downtime is requested.
3. Fill the skewers to the top with chicken, peppers, and onions.
4. Lightly oil the grill grates and set the temperature to medium-high.
5. Cook the skewers on a hot grill, turning regularly, for about 10 to 15 minutes, or until the chicken and veggies are cooked.
6. Serve immediately with your preferred sauce or dip.

Leftover recipe storage: Store in the container and cover it with lid, place the container in the refrigerator.

Leftover recipe reheat/reuse instructions: Take the desired quantity from the refrigerator, heat in the microwave or on a pan and serve.

- Orange juice, fresh - ½ cup
- Lime juice, fresh - ¼ cup
- Canola oil - 2 tbsp.
- Chili powder - 2 tbsp.
- Chicken thighs boneless and skinless, cut half into lengthwise - 6
- Garlic cloves, coarsely chopped - 3
- Salt - according to taste
- Black pepper – according or to taste
- Chipotle in adobo sauce, pureed, optional - 2 tbsp.
- Skewers, either metal or bamboo - 24

1. Mix together the orange juice, lime juice, oil, chili powder, garlic, salt, and pepper in a large mixing basin.
2. Allow the chicken to marinate in the orange juice mixture for 1 to 4 hours, or until cold.
3. Turn on the grill's middle heat setting.
4. Stitch the chicken onto skewers and grill for 4 minutes each side, or until cooked through.
5. Take the chicken off the skewers after grilling, and let it rest for 5 minutes before serving with the yogurt mint sauce.

Leftover recipe storage: Store in the container and cover it with lid, place the container in the refrigerator.

Leftover recipe reheat/reuse instructions: Take the desired quantity from the refrigerator, heat in the microwave or on a pan and serve.

12.10 Chicken Sticks

| per serving | 218 Cal | 9.8g | 3.1g | 27.4g | 0g | 423 mg | 686.6 mg |

- Chicken breasts, boneless and skinless, halves - 4
- Meat tenderizer - 1 tsp.
- Cilantro, optional – for serving

1. Wash and pat dry the chicken under running water.
2. To coat evenly, toss the chicken and meat tenderizer in a large mixing bowl. Allow for 30-60 minutes of resting time.
3. Grill should be heated to medium-high temperatures.
4. Place the chicken pieces on the skewers.
5. Cook for five to ten minutes each side on the grill will do the trick for the chicken skewers.
6. Garnish with cilantro before serving.

Leftover recipe storage: Store in the container and cover it with lid, place the container in the refrigerator.

Leftover recipe reheat/reuse instructions: Take the desired quantity from the refrigerator, heat in the microwave or on a pan and serve.

12.11 Salsa Chicken Sticks

| per serving | 148 Cal | 3.1g | 2.2g | 26.7g | 0.8g | 374 mg | 271.2 mg |

- Salsa - ⅛ cup
- Olive oil - ½ tbsp.
- Garlic, minced - 4 cloves
- Poultry seasoning - ½ tsp.
- Lemon pepper seasoning - ¼ tsp.
- Salsa - ¼ cup
- Chicken breasts, tenderloins - 1 pound
- Skewers - either metal or bamboo

1. Mix together ⅛ cup salsa, garlic, olive oil, lemon pepper seasoning, and poultry seasoning in a large bowl.
2. Set aside for 2 to 24 hours after tossing the chicken in the salsa mixture (refrigerate if sitting for more than 4 hours).
3. Grill should be heated to medium-high temperatures.
4. Prepared chicken should be threaded onto skewers.
5. To ensure that the chicken is cooked through, you should grill the skewers for 8-10 minutes.
6. During the last 2 minutes of grilling, brush the chicken with the remaining ¼ cup salsa.
7. Serve immediately with your preferred sauce or dip.

Leftover recipe storage: Store in the container and cover it with lid, place the container in the refrigerator.

Leftover recipe reheat/reuse instructions: Take the desired quantity from the refrigerator, heat in the microwave or on a pan and serve.

12.12 Grilled Teriyaki chicken cubes

| per serving | 502 Cal | 10g | 48g | 56g | 26.9g | 699 mg | 2554 mg |

- Boneless chicken, cut into 1-inch pieces - 2 pounds
- Soy sauce - ¾ cup
- Brown sugar - ¾ cup
- Pineapple juice - ½ cup
- Garlic, minced - 2 cloves
- Ginger, minced - ½ tsp.
- Skewers - 8
- Salad, optional - for serving

1. Let the chicken marinate for at least an hour after combining it with the first six ingredients (in a big mixing bowl).

2. Lightly oil the grill grates and set the temperature to medium-high.

3. The chicken skewers should be threaded with chicken.

4. The chicken should be grilled for around three to five minutes each side.

5. Serve with salad after removing from the grill.

Leftover recipe storage: Store in the container and cover it with lid, place the container in the refrigerator.

Leftover recipe reheat/reuse instructions: Take the desired quantity from the refrigerator, heat in the microwave or on a pan and serve.

CHAPTER 13
SNACKS AND APPETIZERS

3 | 5" | 30"

13.1 Kale Chips

| per serving | 25 Cal | 24g | 0.9g | 0.5g | 0.2g | 52.4 mg | 30 mg |

- Tuscan kale, washed and dry - 1 bunch
- Kosher salt - ⅛ tsp.
- Onion powder - ¼ tsp.
- Olive oil - ½ tbsp.

1. Put in a preheated 275 degree F oven.
2. Kale leaves may be torn into whichever size chips you choose.
3. Toss the kale leaves with the olive oil in a medium basin.
4. Arrange parchment paper on a large baking sheet.
5. Sprinkle the kale leaves with salt and onion powder, and arrange them in a single layer on a baking sheet.
6. The kale leaves should be baked for 30 to 35 minutes.
7. Allow the kale chips to cool before serving.

Leftover recipe storage: Store in an airtight container, place the container.

Leftover recipe reheat/reuse instructions: Take desired quantity from the container and serve.

10 | 10" | 10"

13.2 Veggie Roll-Ups

| per serving | 33 Cal | 1.6g | 4.2g | 0.9g | 1.3g | 76 mg | 75 mg |

- Spinach, chopped - 1 cup
- Salt - ¼ tsp.
- Pepper - ⅛ tsp.
- Red bell peppers, chopped - 2
- Tortillas - 2
- Cream cheese - 4 tbsp.

1. Spread the cream cheese evenly on both tortillas.
2. Layer spinach, followed by bell pepper.
3. Season the rolls to taste with salt and pepper.
4. Tightly roll the tortillas.
5. Serve the rolled tortillas cut into 5 pieces.

Leftover recipe storage: Store in the container and cover it with lid, place the container in the refrigerator.

Leftover recipe reheat/reuse instructions: Take the desired quantity from the refrigerator, heat in the microwave or on a pan and serve.

- Garlic clove, grated - 1
- Kosher salt - ¾ tsp.
- Frozen edamame in the shell - 1 pound
- Salt for boiling - 1 tbsp.
- Toasted sesame oil - ½ tbsp.
- Water - 2-liter

1. The water and salt should be brought to a boil in a big pot.

2. The water should be boiling when you add the edamame.

3. Cook the edamame in salted water for seven to ten minutes, or until they become a vibrant green and are soft.

4. To prepare the edamame, bring water to a boil in a medium dish.

5. Toss in the toasted sesame oil, garlic, and salt to coat.

6. Serve hot, with a small empty bowl for the pods.

Leftover recipe storage: Store in the container and cover it with lid, place the container in the refrigerator.

Leftover recipe reheat/reuse instructions: Take the desired quantity from the refrigerator, heat in the microwave or on a pan and serve.

- Ripe bananas, thinly sliced - 10
- Lemon juice - 1

1. It's time to turn on the oven and set it to 200 degrees Fahrenheit.

2. Use foil to line a large baking sheet and spray it with oil.

3. Banana slices and lemon juice should be mixed together in a big basin.

4. Spread the bananas out in a single layer on the baking sheet.

5. Keep in the oven for a further 30 minutes if you want the tops to be golden brown. Using a spatula, flip the slices.

6. Bake for 60 minutes more, or until crisp. On a regular basis, check on the chips. (If the chips are sticking and difficult to flip, continue baking for another 20-30 minutes before flipping.)

7. Allow the chips to cool completely before serving with your favorite sauce or dip, if desired.

Leftover recipe storage: Store in a container.

Leftover recipe reheat/reuse instructions: Take the desire quantity from the container, and serve.

13.5 Apple Almond Balls

| per serving | 121 Cal | 5.5g | 17.6g | 2.5g | 13.9g | 182 mg | 43 mg |

- Raw almonds - ½ cup
- Cinnamon, ground - ½ tbsp.
- Apple rings, dried and unsweetened - 1 cup
- Crushed coconut for coating - 1 cup
- Pitted dates, soaked for 15 minutes - 1 cup
- Chocolate protein powder - 1 scoop
- Gala apple, chopped - 1 small
- Nutmeg, ground - ¼ tsp.
- Salt - ⅛ tsp.
- Raw almond butter - 2 tbsp.

1. Blend the apple rings, dates, almonds, almond butter, cinnamon, nutmeg, protein powder, and apple for 1 to 3 minutes, stopping to scrape down the sides of the food processor as required, until completely smooth.

2. Form 14 balls with your hands.

3. Coat the ball in crushed coconut before serving.

Leftover recipe storage: Store in the container and cover it with lid, place the container in the refrigerator.

Leftover recipe reheat/reuse instructions: Take the desire quantity from the refrigerator, and serve.

13.6 Rainbow Rolls

| per serving | 78 Cal | 4.7g | 9.2g | 1.9g | 4.5g | 422 mg | 316 mg |

- Mango, chopped - ¼ cup
- Carrot, chopped - ¼ cup
- Golden beetroot, chopped - ¼ cup
- Black pepper - ¼ tsp.
- Red radish, chopped - ½ cup
- Salt - ½ tsp.
- Avocado, chopped - 1
- Honey - 1 tsp.
- Cabbage, chopped - ¼ cup
- Lemon juice - 2
- Orange juice - 2 tbsp.
- Mix bell peppers, chopped - ½ cup
- Chard leaves - 6-10
- Kitchen threads - 6-10

1. In a large mixing bowl, combine all of the roll ingredients except the chard leaves and threads.

2. Place the chard leaves on a flat surface and set aside.

3. Distribute the roll mixture evenly among the chard and leaves. Fold 1 inch of each side toward the center before rolling up jelly-roll style and tying with kitchen thread.

4. If desired, top with a dollop of your favorite sauce.

Leftover recipe storage: Store in a container with a lid on, and place in the refrigerator.

Leftover recipe reheat/reuse instructions: Take the desire quantity from the refrigerator, and serve

13.7 Crispy Sesame Cauliflower

per serving	305 Cal	15.6g	35.3g	8.2g	18g	701 mg	2233 mg

- Toasted sesame oil - 2 tbsp.
- Sesame seeds for garnish - 2 tbsp.
- Chili paste - 1-2 tbsp.
- Cauliflower
- Sea salt - ¼ tsp.
- Garlic powder - ½ tsp.
- Water - 1 ½ cups
- Cauliflower, florets - 1 ½ pound
- Cassava flour - 1 cup
- Sesame seeds - 1 tbsp.
- Ground black pepper - ⅛ tsp.
- Sauce
- Maple syrup - ¼ cup
- Tamari soy sauce - ½ cup
- Tomato paste - 1 tbsp.
- Green onions, chopped, for garnish - 2
- Rice vinegar - 2 tbsp.
- Garlic, finely minced - 3 cloves
- Ginger, finely minced - 3-inch

1. Turn on the oven to 450 degrees F.
2. Baking parchment paper may be used to line one big baking sheet or two smaller ones.
3. Whisk together the cassava flour, water, garlic powder, sesame seeds, salt, and pepper in a large bowl.
4. Spread the flour mixture evenly over the cauliflower florets.
5. Spread the coated cauliflower florets out on baking pans with a 1-inch gap between each one.
6. Place in oven and bake for 20 minutes at 350 degrees Fahrenheit.
7. In the meanwhile, get the sauce ready. Combine the tamari, maple syrup, sesame oil, rice vinegar, tomato paste, chili paste, garlic, ginger, and sesame seeds in a small saucepan and bring to a simmer.
8. Simmer the sauce for 5 minutes, or until it has been reduced, after bringing it to a boil over medium heat. Putting aside.
9. After 20 minutes, take the cauliflower out of the oven and let it cool down a little.
10. Place the cooked cauliflower and sauce in a large mixing basin.
11. Continue baking for another 15-20 minutes, or until the florets are a deep golden brown and the edges have darkened and the sauce has set.
12. Prepare the cauliflower as directed, topping each serving with more sesame seeds and chopped green onions.

Leftover recipe storage: Store in the container and cover it with lid, place the container in the refrigerator.

Leftover recipe reheat/reuse instructions: Take the desired quantity from the refrigerator, heat in the microwave or on a pan and serve.

13.8 Beet Chips

per serving	164 Cal	14.2g	10.2g	1.8g	4g	157 mg	2402 mg

- Large red beets, thinly sliced - 2
- Ground paprika - ¼ tsp.
- Chili flakes - 1 tsp.
- Olive oil - 2 tbsp.
- Salt - 2 tsp.

1. The oven has to be preheated to 375 degrees Fahrenheit.
2. Prepare two large, parchment-lined baking sheets
3. In a large mixing bowl, combine all of the chip ingredients.
4. Leave a ½-inch space between the beet chips on the prepared baking sheets and bake for 30 minutes.
5. After 30 minutes, decrease oven temperature to 250 degrees Fahrenheit and bake for another 20 to 30 minutes, or until almost crisp.
6. After taking the chips out of the oven, let them cool fully.
7. If desired, serve with your favorite dip or sauce.

Leftover recipe storage: Store in a container.

Leftover recipe reheat/reuse instructions: Take the desire quantity from the container, and serve.

13.9 Chickpea Crackers

per serving	48 Cal	5g	5.1g	2.7g	5.5g	617 mg	426 mg

- Pink salt - ½ tsp.
- Chickpea garbanzo bean flour - 1 cup
- Baking powder - 1 tsp.
- Chives, chopped - 2 tbsp.
- Olive oil - 2 tbsp.
- Sea salt, for sprinkle - ½ tsp.
- Water - 3 tbsp.

1. The oven has to be preheated to 375 degrees F.
2. All of the cracker ingredients should be mixed together in a large bowl.
3. Combine until a ball of dough can be formed.
4. Prepare a parchment paper-lined cutting board.
5. Dust the dough with flour, then turn it out onto a floured piece of parchment paper.
6. Thickness of approximately an eighth of an inch is ideal.
7. Use a knife or pizza cutter to create the appropriate shapes from the dough.
8. Use a damp fork to prick holes all over the top of the formed cracker. Add some salt from the sea to taste.
9. To bake the crackers, lay the parchment paper on which you rolled and cut them on a large baking sheet.
10. Bake in the oven for 20 minutes, or until the crackers are golden and crisp.
11. Allow the crackers to cool completely before breaking them apart and serving.

Leftover recipe storage: Store in a container.

Leftover recipe reheat/reuse instructions: Take the desire quantity from the container, and serve.

- Baking soda - ¼ tsp.
- Buckwheat flour - ¾ cup
- Ground cinnamon - 1 tsp.
- Ground cloves - ⅛ tsp.
- Sea salt - ⅛ tsp.
- Melted coconut oil - 2 tbsp.
- Coconut sugar - 5 tbsp.
- Almond milk - ¼ cup
- Tapioca starch - 6 tbsp.

1. Sift the flour, sugar, spices, and baking soda together in a large basin.
2. Combine the milk and other ingredients well.
3. Knead the dough by hand until it is smooth and elastic and you can shape it into a ball.
4. Cover the dough and chill it for approximately one hour.
5. The oven has to be preheated to 375 degrees Fahrenheit.
6. Prepare a large baking sheet lined with foil or parchment.
7. Place the dough in a parchment-lined baking dish, flatten with your hands, and cover with another sheet of parchment paper.
8. Gently roll out the dough until it is 14-inch or 12-inch thick.
9. Remove the parchment paper top layer.
10. Cut the dough into desired shapes with a knife or pizza cutter.
11. With a fork, prick the cracker tops.
12. Bake in the oven for about 20 minutes, or until the edges are golden.
13. Take the crackers out of the oven and put them on a wire rack to cool. Once they're cold, you can break them apart and serve them.

Leftover recipe storage: Store in a container.

Leftover recipe reheat/reuse instructions: Take the desire quantity from the container, and serve.

- Ground coriander - ¼ tsp.
- Onion powder - ¼ tsp.
- Garlic powder - ½ tsp.
- Ground cumin - ½ tsp.
- Sea salt - ½ tsp.
- Smoked paprika - ½ tsp.
- Ground black pepper - ¼ tsp.
- Chickpeas, rinse and dry - 1 15 oz. Can
- Olive oil - 1 tbsp.

1. Turn on the oven to 400 degrees F.
2. Put parchment paper on a large baking sheet. Putting aside.
3. Mix the paprika, garlic powder, onion powder, sea salt, and black pepper with the cumin in a small bowl. Putting aside.
4. Prepare a baking sheet and spread the chickpeas out on it.
5. Bake for about 15 minutes. (Bake just chickpeas).
6. Take the chickpeas out of the oven and mix them with the olive oil to get a uniform coating. Mix the spices and chickpeas together in a large bowl.
7. Bake for another 10 minutes at 400 degrees. When the timer goes off, take the chickpeas out of the oven and swirl them around.
8. Put the chickpeas back in the oven and for another 5-10 minutes, until they've reached the desired crispiness.
9. Close the oven's door slightly and turn off the heat. So, let the chickpeas cool down.
10. Cooked chickpeas should be served immediately after baking.

Leftover recipe storage: Store in a container.

Leftover recipe reheat/reuse instructions: Take the desired quantity from the container and serve.

- Black pepper - ½ tsp.
- Salt - ½ tsp.
- Feta cheese block, cut into 1-inch cubes - 9 ounces
- Black olives, pitted - 18
- Cherry tomatoes, halved - 9
- Skewers, either metal or bamboo - 18

1. Thread each skewer with a cherry tomato, feta cheese, and olive; make 18
2. Before serving the sticks, season them with some salt and pepper.

Leftover recipe storage: Store in the container and cover it with lid, place the container in the refrigerator.

Leftover recipe reheat/reuse instructions: Take the desire quantity from the refrigerator, and serve.

13.13 Skewered Mushrooms

per serving	46.5 Cal	3.6g	2.5g	2.2g	0.3g	158 mg	296.2 mg

- Black pepper - ¼ tsp.
- Olive oil - 1 ½ tbsp.
- Soy sauce - 1 ½ tbsp.
- Salt - ½ tsp.
- Garlic, minced - 2 cloves
- Thyme, chopped - 1 tsp.
- Fresh parsley, chopped - 1 tbsp.
- Paprika - ½ tsp.
- Portobello mushrooms, halved - 7 ounces
- Skewers - either metal or bamboo
- Mint leaves - for serving

1. Add 1 tbsp. of olive oil, 1 tbsp. of soy sauce, 1 tbsp. each of garlic, thyme, parsley, paprika, salt, and pepper to a large mixing bowl.
2. To coat the mushrooms evenly, toss them in the soy sauce mixture.
3. In a small mixing bowl, combine the remaining soy sauce and olive oil.
4. Preheat the grill to medium-high temperature.
5. Insert the skewers into the mushrooms.
6. Cook for three to four minutes each side on the grill, then turn and coat the mushrooms with the oil and soy sauce.
7. Remove the skewers from the grill and garnish with mint leaves before serving.

Leftover recipe storage: Store in the container and cover it with lid, place the container in the refrigerator.

Leftover recipe reheat/reuse instructions: Take the desired quantity from the refrigerator, heat in the microwave or on a pan and serve.

13.14 Crispy Accordion Potatoes

per serving	448 Cal	27.76 g	46.55 g	5.5g	1.1g	384 mg	236 mg

- Garlic, minced - 1 clove
- Butter - ¼ cup
- Kosher salt - ½ tsp.
- Black pepper, freshly ground - ¼ tsp.
- Foil
- Large potatoes, whole - 4
- Skewers, either metal or bamboo - 4

1. In a small mixing bowl, combine together the pepper, salt, garlic, and butter. Set aside.
2. Cut the potato crosswise, leaving ½ inch at the end attached. Rep with the remaining potatoes.
3. Brush the butter mixture evenly over the potatoes.
4. Wrap aluminum foil around the skewers.
5. Cook the prepared skewers for 45-47 minutes, or until tender and golden brown, over a low to medium flame.
6. Serve immediately.

Leftover recipe storage: Store in the container and cover it with lid, place the container in the refrigerator.

Leftover recipe reheat/reuse instructions: Take the desired quantity from the refrigerator, heat in the microwave or on a pan and serve.

4 · 5" · 7"

13.15 Zucchini Rolls

| per serving | 35.25 Cal | 0.72g | 6.41g | 3.76g | 0.9g | 246 mg | 96.75 mg |

- Smoked salmon slices, cut into half - 8
- Dill strings - 8
- Salt, or to taste - 1 tsp.
- Zucchini, large, cut thing slices lengthwise (make 8 strips) - 2
- Skewers, either metal or bamboo - 8

1. Lightly oil the grill grates and set the temperature to medium-high.
2. Arrange the zucchini strips on a flat surface.
3. Place a slice of smoked salmon on top of the zucchini.
4. Insert the dill string between the salmon and the roll.
5. String the skewers through the rolled zucchini.
6. Sprinkle salt over the zucchini rolls.
7. Cook the skewers for 5-7 minutes on the grill, turning frequently.
8. Serve the skewers hot off the grill.

Leftover recipe storage: Store in the container and cover it with lid, place the container in the refrigerator.

Leftover recipe reheat/reuse instructions: Take the desired quantity from the refrigerator, heat in the microwave or on a pan and serve.

---

6 · 5" · 0"

13.16 Caprese Salad Skewers

| per serving | 85.83 Cal | 6.82g | 1.33g | 4.3g | 0.5g | 49 mg | 57 mg |

- Cherry tomatoes - 12
- Low fat mozzarella cheese ball, cherry size - 12
- Salt - ¼ tsp.
- Skewers, either metal or bamboo - 6
- Olive oil - 1 tbsp.

1. Thread the cherry tomato, then the cheese ball, on the skewers, 2 cherry tomatoes and 2 cheese balls on 1 skewer, and so on until all the skewers are ready.
2. Arrange the skewers on the serving platter.
3. Serve with a little drizzle of olive oil and a sprinkle of salt.

Leftover recipe storage: Store in the container and cover it with lid, place the container in the refrigerator.

Leftover recipe reheat/reuse instructions: Take the desire quantity from the refrigerator, and serve.

- Strawberries, medium - 16
- Whipped cream - 2 cups
- Basic butter cookies - 20
- Skewers, either metal or bamboo - 8

1. Place 1 cookie on the plate, then the whipped cream, then the strawberry, repeat 3 times, and finish with 1 cookie on top.

2. Carefully insert the skewer into the cake tower.

3. Make three more skewers and serve.

Leftover recipe storage: Store in the container and cover it with lid, place the container in the refrigerator.

Leftover recipe reheat/reuse instructions: Take the desire quantity from the refrigerator, and serve.

- Lemon zest - ½ tsp.
- Red pepper flakes, crushed - ¼ tsp.
- Medium zucchini, sliced into strips - 2
- Basil leaves, torn - 4
- Freshly ground black pepper - according to taste
- Extra-virgin olive oil - 1 tbsp.
- Kosher salt - according to taste

1. Preheat the grill to medium-high. Combine the zucchini, oil, lemon zest, and red pepper flakes in a large mixing bowl. Season the zucchini to taste with salt and pepper.

2. When the grill is hot, lightly wipe the grates with tongs and an oiled paper towel.

3. Grill both sides of the zucchini. With the lid on, grill for 3-5 minutes. Cook for another two to three minutes on high with the lid on.

4. Before serving, remove the zucchini from the heat, mix in the basil, and season with additional red pepper flakes.

Leftover recipe storage: Store in the container and cover it with lid, place the container in the refrigerator.

Leftover recipe reheat/reuse instructions: Take the desired quantity from the refrigerator, heat in the microwave or on a pan and serve.

13.19 Onion Rings

| per serving | 137 Cal | 1.6g | 26.6g | 4.3g | 3.5g | 161 mg | 282 mg |

- Paprika - ½ tsp.
- Salt - ½ tsp.
- Turmeric - ¼ tsp.
- Yellow onions - 2–3
- Unsweetened plant milk - 2/3 cup
- Panko bread crumbs - 1 cup
- All purpose flour - ½ cup
- Paprika - ½ tsp.
- Turmeric - ¼ tsp.
- Salt - ¼ tsp.

1. To bake well, the oven has to be preheated to 450 degrees F.

2. You should peel each onion after slicing off the root end. Cut each onion into half-inch slices using a sharp knife.

3. Combine all of the Wet Mix ingredients in a medium mixing basin and whisk well.

4. In a separate bowl, properly combine all of the dry mix ingredients.

5. Then, divide the dry mix equally between the two bowls. (The Dry Mix becomes a little "sticky" over time, which keeps it from becoming useless.)

6. Each Onion Ring should be dipped in the Wet Mix, then moved to the Dry Mix and evenly coated with breadcrumbs.

7. On a silicone mat, bake the onion rings for 30-35 minutes. If you use parchment paper, you may want to flip the rings, but otherwise you should be fine. Warm is preferable.

Leftover recipe storage: Store in the container and cover it with lid, place the container in the refrigerator.

Leftover recipe reheat/reuse instructions: Take the desired quantity from the refrigerator, heat in the microwave or on a pan and serve.

13.20 Avocado Fries

| per serving | 180 Cal | 10.6g | 20.1g | 3.6g | 2g | 262 mg | 505 mg |

- Ground cumin - ½ tsp.
- Salt - ½ tsp.
- Panko breadcrumbs - ¾ cup
- Hass avocado, peeled, pitted, and sliced - 1
- Aquafaba, liquid from can beans - ½ cup
- Garlic powder - 1 tsp.
- Onion powder - 1 tsp.

1. In a small bowl, mix the panko, salt, and seasonings together. Spread aquafaba halfway in a second, smaller dish.

2. Spread an equal coating of panko bread crumbs over the avocado slices. Avocados may be made crunchier by pressing panko into the slices.

3. Turn on the oven to 400 degrees F. Spread the fries in a single layer on a baking sheet coated with butter paper, leaving little space between them. Please avoid touching each other! Without turning, bake for 20 to 23 minutes. They are done when they turn golden brown.

4. Serve immediately with your favorite dipping sauce.

Leftover recipe storage: Store in the container and cover it with lid, place the container in the refrigerator.

Leftover recipe reheat/reuse instructions: Take the desired quantity from the refrigerator, heat in the microwave or on a pan and serve.

CHAPTER 14

SMOOTHIES

14.1 Broccoli Smoothie

per serving	220 Cal	24.5g	20.1g	5.7g	25.7g	1126 mg	93 mg

- Raw broccoli florets - 1 cup
- Dairy-free plain yogurt - ½ cup
- Kale - ½ cup
- Almond milk, unsweetened - ½ cup
- Fresh leaf spinach - 1 cup

1. Fill a blender halfway with the smoothie ingredients.
2. Blend the mixture for 2-3 minutes, or until smooth and creamy.
3. Serve the creamy smoothie in serving glasses.

Leftover recipe storage: Store in a jar or glass in the refrigerator with or without a lid.

Leftover recipe reheat/reuse instructions: Take the desired quantity from the jar/glass and serve.

14.2 Green Smoothie

per serving	198 Cal	10g	25.9g	5.4g	5.8g	1076 mg	198 mg

- Coconut milk - 1/3 cup
- Agave syrup - 1 tbsp.
- Bottle ground - 1 cup
- Coconut water - 1 cup
- Kale - 2 handfuls
- Spinach - 2 handfuls
- Lime juice - ½

1. Fill a blender halfway with the smoothie ingredients.
2. Blend the mixture for 2-3 minutes, or until smooth and creamy.
3. Serve the creamy smoothie in serving glasses.

Leftover recipe storage: Store in a jar or glass in the refrigerator with or without a lid.

Leftover recipe reheat/reuse instructions: Take the desired quantity from the jar/glass and serve.

14.3 Pumpkin Smoothie

| per serving | 352 Cal | 3.9g | 67.2g | 14.1g | 45.5g | 1169 mg | 149 mg |

- Pumpkin puree - ½ cup
- Large banana - 1
- Agave nectar - 1
- Milk - 3 tbsp.
- Vanilla yogurt - 6 oz.
- Ice cubes - 6-8
- Pumpkin pie spice - ½ tsp.

1. Fill a blender halfway with the smoothie ingredients.
2. Blend the mixture for 2-3 minutes, or until smooth and creamy.
3. Serve the creamy smoothie in serving glasses.

Leftover recipe storage: Store in a jar or glass in the refrigerator with or without a lid.

Leftover recipe reheat/reuse instructions: Take the desired quantity from the jar/glass and serve.

14.4 Kale Smoothie

| per serving | 109 Cal | 0.4g | 21.4g | 6.4g | 8.3g | 777 mg | 119 mg |

- Zucchini, chopped - ½ cup
- Coconut water - ¼ cup
- Peas - ¼ cup
- Kale leaves - 1 cup
- Maple syrup - ½ tsp.
- Plant-based greek yogurt - 1/3 cup

1. Fill a blender halfway with the smoothie ingredients.
2. Blend the mixture for 2-3 minutes, or until smooth and creamy.
3. Serve the creamy smoothie in serving glasses.

Leftover recipe storage: Store in a jar or glass in the refrigerator with or without a lid.

Leftover recipe reheat/reuse instructions: Take the desired quantity from the jar/glass and serve.

14.5 Beet Smoothie

per serving	627 Cal	59.7g	23.4g	8.8g	13.8g	1069 mg	116 mg

- Coconut milk, unsweetened - 1 cup
- Medium beetroot, chopped - 1
- Ground flaxseed - 1 tbsp.
- Baby spinach leaves - handful

1. Fill a blender halfway with the smoothie ingredients.
2. Blend the mixture for 2-3 minutes, or until smooth and creamy.
3. Serve the creamy smoothie in serving glasses.

Leftover recipe storage: Store in a jar or glass in the refrigerator with or without a lid.

Leftover recipe reheat/reuse instructions: Take the desired quantity from the jar/glass and serve.

14.6 Spinach Smoothie

per serving	226 Cal	12.5g	23.1g	18g	2.6g	631 mg	69 mg

- Leeks - ½ cup
- Baby spinach - 2 cups
- Mint leaves - 2 tbsp.
- Parsley - 2 tbsp.
- Almond milk, unsweetened - 1 cup
- Chia seeds - 2 tsp.

1. Fill a blender halfway with the smoothie ingredients.
2. Blend the mixture for 2-3 minutes, or until smooth and creamy.
3. Serve the creamy smoothie in serving glasses.

Leftover recipe storage: Store in a jar or glass in the refrigerator with or without a lid.

Leftover recipe reheat/reuse instructions: Take the desired quantity from the jar/glass and serve.

14.7 Celery Smoothie

per serving	88 Cal	2.2g	15.1g	2.8g	3.4g	1347 mg	352 mg

- Ginger, grated - 1 tsp.
- Baby spinach - 1 cup
- Cauliflower florets - 1 cup
- Frozen celery, chopped - 1 cup
- Oat milk - 1 cup
- Lemon juice - 1 tbsp

1. SFill a blender halfway with the smoothie ingredients.
2. Blend the mixture for 2-3 minutes, or until smooth and creamy.
3. Serve the creamy smoothie in serving glasses.

Leftover recipe storage: Store in a jar or glass in the refrigerator with or without a lid.

Leftover recipe reheat/reuse instructions: Take the desired quantity from the jar/glass and serve.

14.8 Sweet Potato Smoothie

per serving	515 Cal	16.9g	62.9g	35.6g	16g	1245 mg	387 mg

- Cashews, roasted - ¼ cup
- Sweet potato, roasted - 1 cup
- Water, chilled - 1 cup
- Vanilla protein powder - 1 scoop
- Sea salt - ⅛ tsp.
- Cinnamon stick - 2 inches

1. Fill a blender halfway with the smoothie ingredients.
2. Blend the mixture for 2-3 minutes, or until smooth and creamy.
3. Serve the creamy smoothie in serving glasses.

Leftover recipe storage: Store in a jar or glass in the refrigerator with or without a lid.

Leftover recipe reheat/reuse instructions: Take the desired quantity from the jar/glass and serve.

14.9 Peach Smoothie

	per serving	462 Cal	30.6g	45.3g	10.3g	32.2g	858 mg	55 mg

- Plant-based Greek yogurt - ¼ cup
- Cinnamon - ¼ tsp.
- Maple syrup - ½ tbsp.
- Vanilla extract - ½ tsp.
- Banana, sliced - 1
- Almond milk - 1 cup
- Frozen peaches, sliced - 2 cups
- Ice cubes - 6

1. Fill a blender halfway with the smoothie ingredients.
2. Blend the mixture for 2-3 minutes, or until smooth and creamy.
3. Serve the creamy smoothie in serving glasses.

Leftover recipe storage: Store in a jar or glass in the refrigerator with or without a lid.

Leftover recipe reheat/reuse instructions: Take the desired quantity from the jar/glass and serve.

14.10 Mixed Smoothie

	per serving	268 Cal	1.3g	65.1g	2.7g	46.2g	680 mg	8 mg

- Maple syrup - 1 tbsp.
- Banana, sliced - 1
- Frozen mango cubes - 1 cup
- Water - 1 cup
- Large green apple, chopped - 1
- Lemon juice - 1 tbsp.
- Mixed berries - 2 cups
- Ice cubes - 10

1. Fill a blender halfway with the smoothie ingredients.
2. Blend the mixture for 2-3 minutes, or until smooth and creamy.
3. Serve the creamy smoothie in serving glasses.

Leftover recipe storage: Store in a jar or glass in the refrigerator with or without a lid.

Leftover recipe reheat/reuse instructions: Take the desired quantity from the jar/glass and serve.

14.11 Orange Smoothie

per serving	310 Cal	1.2g	73.5g	6.7g	51.4g	1175 mg	25 mg

- Orange zest - ½ tbsp.
- Vanilla extract - ½ tsp.
- Banana, sliced - 1
- Maple syrup - 1 tbsp.
- Large oranges, peeled - 2
- Plant-based Greek yogurt - ¼ cup
- Ice - 2 to 2 ½ cups

1. Fill a blender halfway with the smoothie ingredients.
2. Blend the mixture for 2-3 minutes, or until smooth and creamy.
3. Serve the creamy smoothie in serving glasses.

Leftover recipe storage: Store in a jar or glass in the refrigerator with or without a lid.

Leftover recipe reheat/reuse instructions: Take the desired quantity from the jar/glass and serve.

14.12 Raspberry Smoothie

per serving	486 Cal	15.1g	90.1g	4.7g	70.7g	713 mg	25 mg

- Almond milk - ½ cup
- Ice - ½ cup
- Water - ½ cup
- Banana, sliced - 1
- Maple syrup - 1 tbsp.
- Plant-based Greek yogurt - ¼ cup
- Frozen raspberries - 2 cups

1. Fill a blender halfway with the smoothie ingredients.
2. Blend the mixture for 2-3 minutes, or until smooth and creamy.
3. Serve the creamy smoothie in serving glasses.

Leftover recipe storage: Store in a jar or glass in the refrigerator with or without a lid.

Leftover recipe reheat/reuse instructions: Take the desired quantity from the jar/glass and serve.

14.13 Apple Smoothie

| per serving | 266 Cal | 8g | 50.8g | 2.9g | 35.7g | 580 mg | 19 mg |

- Cinnamon - ¼ tsp.
- Plant-based greek yogurt - ½ cup
- Maple syrup - ½ tbsp.
- Vanilla extract - ½ tsp.
- Ripe banana, sliced - 1
- Apple chunks - 2 cups
- Almond milk - ¼ cup
- Ice cubes - 8

1. Fill a blender halfway with the smoothie ingredients.
2. Blend the mixture for 2-3 minutes, or until smooth and creamy.
3. Serve the creamy smoothie in serving glasses.

Leftover recipe storage: Store in a jar or glass in the refrigerator with or without a lid.

Leftover recipe reheat/reuse instructions: Take the desired quantity from the jar/glass and serve.

14.14 Choco Berry Smoothie

| per serving | 407 Cal | 9.7g | 76.6g | 10.8g | 32.3g | 573 mg | 44 mg |

- Cocoa powder - ¼ cup
- Oat milk - ¾ cup
- Banana, sliced - 1
- Frozen strawberries - 1 cup
- Old-fashioned oats - ½ cup
- Ice - 1 cup
- Almond butter - 1 tbsp.
- Maple syrup - 2 tbsp.

1. Fill a blender halfway with the smoothie ingredients.
2. Blend the mixture for 2-3 minutes, or until smooth and creamy.
3. Serve the creamy smoothie in serving glasses.

Leftover recipe storage: Store in a jar or glass in the refrigerator with or without a lid.

Leftover recipe reheat/reuse instructions: Take the desired quantity from the jar/glass and serve.

- Plant-based Greek yogurt - ½ cup
- Cinnamon - ½ tsp.
- Large ripe banana, sliced - 1
- Medium carrot, chopped - 1
- Frozen blueberries - 2 cups
- Water - 2 tbsp.

1. Fill a blender halfway with the smoothie ingredients.

2. Blend the mixture for 2-3 minutes, or until smooth and creamy.

3. Serve the creamy smoothie in serving glasses.

Leftover recipe storage: Store in a jar or glass in the refrigerator with or without a lid.

Leftover recipe reheat/reuse instructions: Take the desired quantity from the jar/glass and serve.

CHAPTER 15

DRINKS

15.1 Chocolate Frappuccino

per serving	114 Cal	2.4g	20.1g	4.5g	15.6g	248 mg	65 mg

- Ice - 3-5 cubes
- Cocoa powder - 1 tsp.
- Soy milk - ½ cup
- Agave nectar - 1 tsp.
- Black coffee - ½ cup

1. Combine together all of the ingredients in a blender and blend until the desired consistency is reached.

2. Pour milk into a separate cup.

3. Fill a glass halfway with black coffee.

4. A large scoop of coconut cream should be placed on top.

5. Serve with sugar-free dark chocolate sauce.

Leftover recipe storage: Store in a jar or glass in the refrigerator with or without a lid.

Leftover recipe reheat/reuse instructions: Take the desired quantity from the jar/glass and serve.

15.2 Green Tea

per serving	16 Cal	0g	5g	0.2g	3.2g	109.1 mg	7.7 mg

- Water - 4 cups
- Lemon peel strips - 4
- Orange peel strips - 4
- Green tea bags - 4
- Raw honey - 2 tsp.
- Lemon slices - 4

1. Peel the lemons and oranges and add them to the water in a medium saucepan. Cook until it boils, then turn off the heat. Leave the lid off and let it cook for 10 minutes. Take a slotted spoon and take off the citrus peels.

2. The tea bags should be tossed into a teapot and the water should be brought to a simmer very away after they have been added. Tea should be steeped in a covered container for the recommended amount of time (1 to 3 minutes). Gently squeeze the tea bags to remove them. Put the tea bags in the trash. Honey should be included into the mixture. Distribute the tea among four glasses or mugs that can withstand heat, and then place a lemon slice on top of each. Distribute immediately.

Leftover recipe storage: Store in a jar or glass in the refrigerator with or without a lid.

Leftover recipe reheat/reuse instructions: Take the desired quantity from the jar/glass and serve.

15.3 Garlic tea

per serving	136 Cal	0.1g	36g	0.4g	35.2g	51 mg	5 mg

- Water - 3 cups
- Garlic cloves, cut in half - 3
- Honey - ½ cup
- Fresh lemon juice - ½ cup

1. In a saucepan, bring 3 cups of water and 3 garlic cloves to a boil. Remove from the heat when the water begins to boil and stir in ½ cup of honey and ½ cup of fresh lemon juice. Strain.

Leftover recipe storage: Store in a jar or glass in the refrigerator with or without a lid.

Leftover recipe reheat/reuse instructions: Take the desired quantity from the jar/glass and serve.

15.4 Lime Iced Tea

per serving	120 Cal	1g	33g	1g	31g	59 mg	8 mg

- Green tea bags - 2
- Hot water - 1 cup
- Raw honey - 3 ½ tbsp.
- Lime juice - 4 ½ tbsp.
- Ice - ½ cup

1. Brew green tea for 3-5 minutes in hot water, or until desired strength is reached
2. Remove tea bags and stir in honey to combine.
3. Allow it to cool for about 10 to 15 minutes.
4. Mix in the lime juice. Pour into serving glasses over ice and serve.

Leftover recipe storage: Store in a jar or glass in the refrigerator with or without a lid.

Leftover recipe reheat/reuse instructions: Take the desired quantity from the jar/glass and serve.

- Ground coffee - 1 pound
- Almond extract - 2 tbsp.
- Vanilla extract - 2 tbsp.

1. Put some coffee in the bottom of a big jar and seal it up. Put the extracts in and stir. In order to mix the ingredients, cover the container and shake it hard. Keep in a sealed container and keep in a cold, dry, dark place.

2. After that, serve.

Leftover recipe storage: Store in a jar or glass in the refrigerator with or without a lid.

Leftover recipe reheat/reuse instructions: Take the desired quantity from the jar/glass and serve.

CHAPTER 16
DESSERTS

24 — **20"** — **25"**

16.1 Oatmeal Cookies

per serving	91 Cal	3.3g	14.5g	1.5g	g	1347 mg	mg

- Ground cinnamon - 1 tsp.
- Salt - ½ tsp.
- White whole-wheat flour - 1 cup
- Packed light brown sugar - 2/3 cup
- Unsalted butter, melted - 6 tbsp.
- Large egg - 1
- Vanilla extract - 1 ½ tsp.
- Old-fashioned rolled oats - 1 cup
- Baking powder - 1 tsp.
- Raisins - ½ cup

1. Set the oven temperature to 350 degrees Fahrenheit and turn it on. Use very little cooking spray to coat a baking sheet.

2. Mix the flour, baking powder, cinnamon, and salt in a medium basin.

3. Combine the sugar, butter, egg, and vanilla essence in a large bowl. Put in the oats, raisins, and flour mixture and stir them together well with a wooden spoon. Spread batter by level tbsp. onto a baking sheet covered with parchment paper; this recipe yields 12 cookies.

4. Toast the bottom for 12–14 minutes. Remove from baking sheet after 5 minutes and place on wire rack to cool entirely. Keep going with the rest of the batter.

Leftover recipe storage: Store in an airtight container.

Leftover recipe reheat/reuse instructions: Take the desired quantity from the container and serve.

---

12 — **10"** — **15"**

16.2 Peanut Butter Cookies

per serving	133.4 Cal	11.2g	12.4g	5.9g	2g	146 mg	104.6 mg

- Peanut butter - 1 cup
- Sugar-free vanilla extract - 1 tsp.
- Low-calorie natural sweetener - ½ cup 1 egg

1. Get the oven up to temperature, preferably 350 degrees Fahrenheit. Get out some parchment paper and prepare a baking sheet.

2. Stir the peanut butter, sugar, egg, and vanilla extract together in a large bowl until a dough forms.

3. Roll the dough into 1 inch balls and repeat 12 times. Crisscross twice with a fork and arrange on a baking sheet covered with parchment paper.

4. Pre-heat the oven to 400 degrees and bake for 12-15 minutes, or until the edges are brown. Transfer to a wire rack to cool for an additional minute when they have cooled for a minute.

Leftover recipe storage: Store in an airtight container.

Leftover recipe reheat/reuse instructions: Take the desired quantity from the container and serve.

- Ground cloves - ¼ tsp.
- Crust
- Almonds - 1 cup
- Pecans - 1 cup
- Ground ginger - ½ tsp.
- Granular sucralose sweetener - 2 (1 gram) packets
- Vanilla extract - 1 tsp.
- Butter, melted - 3 tbsp.
- Filling
- Low-fat cream cheese, at room temperature - 3 (8 ounce) packages
- Granular sucralose sweetener - 2/3 cup
- Pumpkin puree - 1 (15 ounce) can
- Ground cinnamon - 1 tsp.
- Salt - ¼ tsp.
- Eggs - 3

1. Preheat the oven to 350 degrees Fahrenheit.

2. Combine almonds and pecans in a food processor until ground but not paste-like. To combine, pulse in the sweetener and butter. Halfway fill a 9-inch springform pan with the mixture.

3. Bake for 10 minutes, or until the crust has turned golden brown. Allow for a 10-minute cooling period.

4. Mix for 2 to 3 minutes in a food processor or with an electric mixer, combine cream cheese and 2/3 cup sweetener until smooth. For another 2 minutes, or until smooth, combine the pumpkin, vanilla extract, cinnamon, ginger, cloves, and salt. Add the eggs one at a time, mixing thoroughly after each addition. The prepared crust should be poured with the filling.

5. Bake for approximately 45 to 50 minutes in a preheated oven, until the center is just set, or the filling jiggles but does not run. Allow 30 minutes for the mixture to cool completely. Refrigerate the cheesecake for at least 4 hours, wrapped in plastic wrap.

Leftover recipe storage: Store in an airtight container, and place the container in the refrigerator.

Leftover recipe reheat/reuse instructions: Take desired quantity from the container and serve.

16.4 Chocolate Mousse

| | per serving | 373.4 Cal | 37.6g | 6.9g | 5.4g | 1g | 234 mg | 227.2 mg |

- Heavy cream - ½ cup
- Vanilla extract - 1 tsp.
- Powdered zero-calorie sweetener - ¼ cup
- Cocoa powder - 2 tbsp.
- Low fat cream cheese, softened - 3 ounces
- Salt - 1 pinch

1. Cream cheese should be beaten with an electric mixer until it is light and frothy in a large mixing basin. Combine the heavy cream and vanilla extract and blend carefully on low speed.

2. Mix in the sweetener, cocoa powder, and salt until thoroughly combined. Mix on high for 1 to 2 minutes more, or until light and fluffy.

3. Refrigerate for later use or serve immediately.

Leftover recipe storage: Store in an airtight container, and place the container in the refrigerator.

Leftover recipe reheat/reuse instructions: Take desired quantity from the container and serve.

16.5 Almond Butter Cookies

| | per serving | 196.3 Cal | 18.4g | 12.7g | 5g | 1g | 9 mg | 60.4 mg |

- Butter, softened - ½ cup
- Egg - 1
- Low-calorie natural sweetener - ½ cup
- Sugar-free vanilla extract - 1 tsp.
- Blanched almond flour - 2 cups
- Ground cinnamon - 1 tsp.

1. Prepare a 350F oven.
2. Get out some parchment paper and prepare a baking sheet.
3. Mix together the almond flour, butter, egg, sugar, vanilla essence, and cinnamon in a large mixing dish.
4. Roll the dough into golf ball-sized pieces. Crisscross twice with a fork and arrange on a baking sheet covered with parchment paper.
5. Bake for 12-15 minutes in a preheated oven, or until the edges are golden brown. Remove from baking sheet after 1 minute and let cool fully on wire rack.

Leftover recipe storage: Store in an airtight container.

Leftover recipe reheat/reuse instructions: Take the desired quantity from the container and serve.

16.6 Rhubarb Crunch

- Butter - ¼ cup
- Chopped fresh rhubarb - 4 cups
- Strawberries, hulled and sliced - 1 pint
- Honey - 1 tbsp.
- Rolled oats - 1 cup
- Packed brown sugar - ½ cup
- Ground cinnamon - 1 tsp.

1. The oven has to be preheated to 375 degrees F.
2. Toss the rhubarb, strawberries, and honey together in a medium basin. Put into a pie plate or other similar dish. Oats, brown sugar, and cinnamon should all be mixed together in the same bowl. Rub the strawberries with the crumbled butter.
3. In a preheated oven, bake for 40 minutes, or until the rhubarb is soft and the topping is browned. In a hot dish.

Leftover recipe storage: Store in an airtight container, and place the container in the refrigerator.

Leftover recipe reheat/reuse instructions: Take desired quantity from the container and serve.

16.7 Coconut Cookies

- Salt - ½ tsp.
- Granular sucralose sweetener - ¾ cup
- Butter - ½ cup
- Baking powder - 1 tsp.
- Eggs - 3
- Heavy cream - ½ tbsp.
- Almond milk - 1 tsp.
- Unsweetened coconut flakes - ½ cup
- Baking soda - 1 tsp.
- Coconut flour - 6 tbsp.
- Almond flour - ¼ cup

1. Bake at 350 degrees Fahrenheit, preheated. Get out some parchment paper and prepare a baking sheet.
2. Combine the sugar and butter in a bowl and beat until fluffy. In a large bowl, whisk together the eggs, cream, and almond milk. The sides should be scraped down using a spatula.
3. Combine the salt, baking soda, baking powder, almond flour, coconut flour, coconut flakes, and in a separate basin. The dough may be brought together by gradually incorporating the flour mixture into the butter mixture.
4. Drop heaping tsp. of cookie dough onto prepared baking trays.
5. Put in an oven that has been prepared to 400 degrees and bake for 17 minutes. Baked goods should rest on baking sheet for 3 minutes before being moved to wire rack.

Leftover recipe storage: Store in an airtight container.

Leftover recipe reheat/reuse instructions: Take the desired quantity from the container and serve.

- Butter, melted - 2 tbsp.
- Finely chopped pecans - ½ cup
- Stevia sugar substitute - ½ cup
- Ground cinnamon - ½ tsp.
- Salt - 1 pinch
- Filling
- Pumpkin puree - 1 (15 ounce) can
- Large eggs - 4
- Granular sucralose sweetener - ¾ cup
- Ground ginger - ½ tsp.
- Crust
- Ground nutmeg - ¼ tsp.
- Ground allspice - ¼ tsp.
- Ground cloves - ¼ tsp.

1. Set the oven at 350 degrees Fahrenheit to preheat.

2. Melt the butter and stir in the pecans, stevia, cinnamon, and salt. Get out a 10-inch pie pan and make a crust for the bottom.

3. Put the pie crust in an oven that has been preheated for 5 minutes. Take the dish out of the oven and turn the heat up to 425 degrees Fahrenheit.

4. Combine the pumpkin puree, eggs, sugar, ginger, nutmeg, allspice, and cloves in a mixing dish. When making a pie, the filling should be put into the crust.

5. Put it in a hot oven for 15 minutes to bake. Drop to a temperature of 350 degrees Fahrenheit and for another 50-60 minutes, or until a knife inserted in the center of the pie comes out clean, the oven should be left uncovered. Wait an hour for cooling time before putting in the fridge. Preserve in the fridge for at least two hours, preferably three.

Leftover recipe storage: Store in an airtight container, and place the container in the refrigerator.

Leftover recipe reheat/reuse instructions: Take desired quantity from the container and serve.

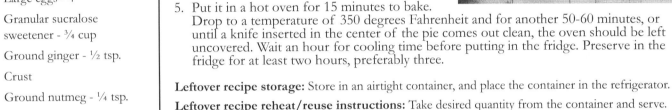

- Baking soda - ¼ tsp.
- Salt - ½ tsp.
- Square unsweetened chocolate - 1 (1 ounce)
- Granular sucralose sweetener - ½ cup
- Water, or as needed - ½ cup
- Butter, melted - ¼ cup
- Egg - 1
- Soy flour - ¼ cup
- Mayonnaise, optional - 1 tsp.
- Vanilla extract - ½ tsp.

1. The oven has to be preheated to 325 degrees Fahrenheit. A tiny muffin tray with 18 cavities has to be lined with paper liners.

2. The chocolate should be melted in 15-second intervals over the course of 1 to 3 minutes in a microwave-safe glass or ceramic dish with stirring in between.

3. Melt the chocolate, then add the sugar, water, butter, and egg to a mixing bowl. Keep stirring until all the sugar has dissolved. Soy flour, mayonnaise, vanilla extract, salt, and baking soda should all be combined in a bowl. Remove any remaining lumps by vigorously whisking. Only use enough batter to fill the muffin cups about halfway.

4. Bake fo about 18 to 21 minutes.

5. Whether you want a fudgy brownie cake, put a toothpick in the middle and see if it comes out clean after 18 to 21 minutes in the ove, then serve.

Leftover recipe storage: Store in an airtight container, and place the container in the refrigerator.

Leftover recipe reheat/reuse instructions: Take desired quantity from the container and serve.

16.10 Strawberry Nice Cream

| per serving | 191 Cal | 0.5g | 22.5g | 1.4g | 12.9g | 388.8 mg | 2.2 mg |

- Ice-cold water, as needed - ¼ cup
- Fresh strawberries, chopped - 1 pound
- Bananas, chopped - 2 medium
- Fresh lemon juice - 1 tbsp.

1. The strawberries and bananas should be placed on separate sheets of baking paper or on opposing sides of a single sheet. Put in the freezer for 12 hours to make sure it becomes firm.

2. Strawberry freeze-thaw time is 15 minutes at room temperature. Put in the machine and pulse 10 times, or until the ingredients are finely minced.

3. Blend for 1 to 1 ½ minutes, pausing to scrape down bowl as required, until desired consistency is reached. May need up to ¼ cup cold water.

4. Serve right away, or store in an airtight container and freeze for up to 30 minutes to firm up the consistency.

Leftover recipe storage: Store in an airtight container, place the container in freezer.

Leftover recipe reheat/reuse instructions: Take desired quantity from the container and serve.

16.11 Meringue cookies

| per serving | 62 Cal | 0.2g | 15g | 0.8g | 7.4g | 6.2 mg | 12.4 mg |

- Confectioners' sugar - 2 ¼ cups
- Egg whites - 4

1. Turn the oven temperature up to 200 degrees Fahrenheit.

2. Rub butter and flour onto a baking sheet.

3. Using an electric mixer, beat the egg whites in a metal or glass bowl until they form stiff peaks. Sprinkle the sugar in gradually while whipping at a medium speed. When the texture of the mixture resembles firm satin, stop mixing and fill a big pastry bag with it. The meringue should be piped onto the prepared baking sheet using a big round or star tip.

4. Put the meringues in the oven and prop the door open with a wooden spoon handle. If you want your meringues to be dry and easy to remove from the pan, bake them for at least three hours. Cookies should be stored at room temperature in an airtight container once they have cooled fully.

Leftover recipe storage: Store in an airtight container.

Leftover recipe reheat/reuse instructions: Take the desired quantity from the container and serve.

16.12 Berry Ice Pops

| per serving | 83.4 Cal | 1.1g | 15.8g | 3.5g | 14.2g | 171.4 mg | 43.2 mg |

- Fresh mixed berries - 2 cups
- Plain or vanilla yogurt - 2 cups
- White sugar - ¼ cup
- Popsicle sticks - 8 small
- Popsicle mold - 8

1. In a blender, combine the blueberries, raspberries, strawberries, sliced bananas, yogurt, and sugar. Cover and blend until the fruit is chunky or smooth to your liking.

2. Fill popsicle mold halfway with the fruit mixture. Wrap a strip of aluminum foil around the top of each cup. To make popsicles, poke a stick through the cellophane of each cup.

3. Refrigerate the cups for at least 5 hours. Remove the foil and the paper cup before serving.

Leftover recipe storage: Store in an airtight container, place the container in freezer.

Leftover recipe reheat/reuse instructions: Take desired quantity from the container and serve.

16.13 Gingerbread Cake

| per serving | 83 Cal | 3.2g | 12.5g | 1.2g | 4.9g | 104.7 mg | 54.2 mg |

- Ground cloves - ¼ tsp.
- Salt - ¼ tsp.
- Baking soda - ½ tsp.
- Ground cinnamon - 1 tsp.
- Ground ginger - 1 tsp.
- Baking powder - 1 ½ tsp.
- All-purpose flour - 2 1/3 cups
- Canola oil - ½ cup
- Granulated sugar - ¼ cup
- Cold water - 1 ¼ cups
- Full-flavor molasses - 2/3 cup
- Eggs, lightly beaten - 2
- Confectioners' sugar - for dusting
- Fresh mint - for garnish

1. Preheat the oven to 350°F. Prepare a 13-by-9-by-2-inch baking dish by gently sprinkling it with nonstick cooking spray. Combine the dry ingredients in a large mixing bowl: cloves, salt, flour, baking soda, cinnamon, ginger, and baking powder.

2. Oil and sugar should be mixed together in a large mixing dish. Add the cold water, molasses, and eggs and whisk until mixed. The flour and water combination that was set aside should be incorporated all at once, and whisked until smooth. Toss into the dish you'll be baking in.

3. A wooden skewer inserted towards the middle should come out clean after 40 to 45 minutes in the oven to bake. Rest wire rack-bound during the duration of cooling. Sprinkle confectioners' sugar over top and, optionally, decorate with raspberries.

Leftover recipe storage: Store in an airtight container, and place the container in the refrigerator.

Leftover recipe reheat/reuse instructions: Take desired quantity from the container and serve.

- Water - 1 cup
- Unsalted butter - 4 tbsp.
- Packed light brown sugar - 2 tbsp.
- Salt - ½ tsp.
- All-purpose flour - 1 cup
- Large eggs - 2
- Vanilla extract - 1 tsp.
- Granulated sugar - 3 tbsp.
- Ground cinnamon - ½ tsp.

1. Set the oven temperature to 375 degrees Fahrenheit. Prepare a baking sheet with a silicone baking mat or parchment paper.

2. Put the water, butter, brown sugar, and salt in a medium pot. Over medium heat, melt the butter and bring the mixture to a boil. Lower the temperature immediately. Use a wooden spoon to stir in the flour until it is well integrated and the sauce starts to leave the edges of the pan. Set aside for 5 minutes to cool.

3. Eggs and vanilla essence should be combined in a separate small basin. Knead it into the dough until it's all integrated. Put the dough in a pastry bag fitted with a ¾-inch open star tip. (Or, if you have a sealable plastic bag that holds 1 quart, fill it nearly to the top with dough and seal it almost fully, leaving a tiny space at the top for air to escape as you press.) Cut the bottom corner off, leaving a ¾-inch hole. Create 12 churros measuring 4 inches in length by piping the dough onto the prepared baking sheet.

4. The churros need to be baked for 25-30 minutes, until they are puffed and browned on both sides.

5. Stir together the sugar and cinnamon in a wide, shallow dish. The churros should be rolled in the mixture while still hot, then let to cool for 10 minutes on a wire rack.

Leftover recipe storage: Store in an airtight container.

Leftover recipe reheat/reuse instructions: Take desired quantity from the container and serve.

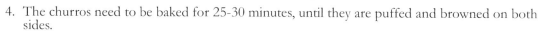

- Natural peanut butter - ½ cup
- Crispy rice cereal - ¾ cup
- Pure maple syrup - 1 tsp.
- Dark chocolate chips, melted - ½ cup

1. Prepare a baking sheet by covering it with parchment paper or wax paper. Combine the peanut butter, cereal, and maple syrup in a medium mixing basin. Roll the ingredients into 12 equal-sized balls using approximately 2 tbsp. for each. Prepare a baking sheet and set the items there. Place the balls in the freezer for approximately 15 minutes, or until they are hard.

2. Roll the chocolate balls in melted chocolate. Return to the freezer for about 15 minutes, or until the chocolate has set.

Leftover recipe storage: Store in an airtight container, and place the container in the refrigerator.

Leftover recipe reheat/reuse instructions: Take desired quantity from the container and serve.

CHAPTER 17

10 WEEKS MEAL PLAN

10 Weeks Meal Plan For Fatty Liver

Week 1

Timing	Monday/Wednesday/Friday	Tuesday/Saturday	Thursday/Sunday
Breakfast	Ingredients Mint - ½ cup Apple - 1 Fresh turmeric - 1-inch Ginger - 1-inch Lemon - 1	Ingredients Kale - 3 leaves Celery, leaves removed - 2 stalks Green apple, halved - 1 Cucumber - ½ Lemon, peeled - ¼ Fresh ginger - ½ inch piece	Ingredients Lemon - peeled, seeded, and quartered - 1 Carrot, chopped - 1 Apples quartered - 1 Beet, trimmed and chopped - 1
	Preparation Following the manufacturer's instructions, put all the ingredients through a juicer and serve with or without ice.	Preparation Following the manufacturer's instructions, put all the ingredients through a juicer and serve with or without ice.	Preparation Following the manufacturer's instructions, put all the ingredients through a juicer and serve with or without ice.
	Calories: 253	Calories: 144	Calories: 158
Dinner	Ingredients Organic carrots, trimmed and scrubbed - ½ pound Organic oranges, peeled - 2	Ingredients Orange, peeled - 1 Lemon, peeled - ½ Green apple, quartered - ½ Fresh spinach - ½ cup Leaf kale - ½	Ingredients Carrots, trimmed - 4 Apples, quartered - 2 Stalks celery - 2 Piece fresh ginger - ½ inch
	Preparation Following the manufacturer's instructions, put all the ingredients through a juicer and serve with or without ice.	Preparation Following the manufacturer's instructions, put all the ingredients through a juicer and serve with or without ice.	Preparation Following the manufacturer's instructions, put all the ingredients through a juicer and serve with or without ice.
	Calories: 183	Calories: 44	Calories: 277

Week 2

Timing	Monday/Wednesday/Friday	Tuesday/Saturday	Thursday/Sunday
Breakfast	Ingredients Chopped hearts of romaine - ½ cup Chopped fresh chives - 2 tbsp. Large tomatoes, cut into wedges - 2 Fresh jalapeño, stemmed and seeded - 2 tbsp. Large red bell pepper, cut into eighths - ½ Large stalk celery, trimmed - 1 Medium carrot, peeled - ½	Ingredients Medium orange, peeled and quartered - ½ Kale leaves - 1 ½ Medium apple, cut into wedges - ½ Medium carrot, peeled - ½ Large beet, peeled and cut into wedges - ½ Peeled fresh ginger - ½ inch	Ingredients Fresh parsley - ¼ cup spinach - 1 ½ Lemon, peeled - ¼ Medium pear, cut into eighths - 1 Large stalks celery, trimmed - 3
	Preparation Following the manufacturer's instructions, put all the ingredients through a juicer and serve with or without ice.	Preparation Following the manufacturer's instructions, put all the ingredients through a juicer and serve with or without ice.	Preparation Following the manufacturer's instructions, put all the ingredients through a juicer and serve with or without ice.
	Calories: 46	Calories: 100	Calories: 91
Dinner	Ingredients Fresh strawberries, hulled - 3 Large cucumber, peeled and cut into chunks - ½ Large red apple, cut into eighths - ½ Medium carrot, peeled - 1	Ingredients spinach - ¾ cup grapefruit, peeled, white pith removed - ¼ green apple, cut into eighths - 1 Peeled fresh ginger - ½ inch Large stalk celery - 1	Ingredients Red cabbage, sliced - ⅛ Large cucumber, peeled and cut into chunks - ½ Fresh blueberries - ½ cup Large apple, cut into eighths - ½
	Preparation Following the manufacturer's instructions, put all the ingredients through a juicer and serve with or without ice.	Preparation Following the manufacturer's instructions, put all the ingredients through a juicer and serve with or without ice.	Preparation Following the manufacturer's instructions, put all the ingredients through a juicer and serve with or without ice.
	Calories: 69	Calories: 55	Calories: 77

Week 3

Timing	Monday/Wednesday/Friday	Tuesday/Saturday	Thursday/Sunday
Breakfast	Ingredients Medium yellow tomato, cut into wedges - ½ Medium orange, peeled and quartered - ½ Medium apple, cut into eighths - ½ Large carrots, peeled - 2	Ingredients Lemon, peeled and halved - 1/3 Granny smith apples, stem removed and cut into pieces - 2 ¼ cup chopped peeled fresh ginger ⅛ tsp. cayenne pepper, plus more for garnish ⅛ tsp. salt	Ingredients Carrots, very coarsely chopped - ¾ cup Fresh turmeric, peeled and coarsely chopped - ½ inch Fresh ginger, peeled and coarsely chopped - ½ inch Unsweetened coconut water, divided 1 ½ tbsp. Salt - pinch
	Preparation Following the manufacturer's instructions, put all the ingredients through a juicer and serve with or without ice.	Preparation Following the manufacturer's instructions, put all the ingredients through a juicer and serve with or without ice.	Preparation Following the manufacturer's instructions, put all the ingredients through a juicer and serve with or without ice.
	Calories: 11	Calories: 49	Calories: 59
Dinner	Ingredients Medium red apple, cored and sliced - ¼ packed fresh spinach - 1 cup Roughly chopped celery ¼ cup 1 cup coconut water Lemon juice - 1 tsp.	Ingredients Peeled, seeded and chopped - 2 cups Cucumber - 1 Granny smith apple, peeled and chopped - ½ pure unsweetened coconut water - ½ cup	Ingredients Fresh mint leaves - 2 tbsp. Grapes - ¼ cup Unsweetened pineapple juice - 3 oz
	Preparation Following the manufacturer's instructions, put all the ingredients through a juicer and serve with or without ice.	Preparation Following the manufacturer's instructions, put all the ingredients through a juicer and serve with or without ice.	Preparation Following the manufacturer's instructions, put all the ingredients through a juicer and serve with or without ice.
	Calories: 45	Calories: 93	Calories: 61

Week 4

Timing	Monday/Wednesday/Friday	Tuesday/Saturday	Thursday/Sunday
Breakfast	Ingredients Cucumber with skin on - ½ Handful spinach - ½ handful Celery stalks - 4 Lime - ½ Lemon - ½ Fresh ginger - ½ -inch	Ingredients Orange - 1 Apple - 1 Black grapes - ½ cup Kiwi - 1	Ingredients Plum - 2 Pineapple - 1 cup
	Preparation Following the manufacturer's instructions, put all the ingredients through a juicer and serve with or without ice.	Preparation Following the manufacturer's instructions, put all the ingredients through a juicer and serve with or without ice.	Preparation Following the manufacturer's instructions, put all the ingredients through a juicer and serve with or without ice.
	Calories: 54	Calories: 280	Calories: 143
Dinner	Ingredients Pineapple, peeled - ¼ cup Carrot - 1 Apple - ¼ Lemon - ¼ Lime - ¼	Ingredients Orange - 1 Grapes - ½ cup Pomegranate - ½ Apple - ½ Kiwi - ½ Lemon - ½	Ingredients Apple - ½ Stalks celery - 2 Bunch parsley - ½ bunch
	Preparation Following the manufacturer's instructions, put all the ingredients through a juicer and serve with or without ice.	Preparation Following the manufacturer's instructions, put all the ingredients through a juicer and serve with or without ice.	Preparation Following the manufacturer's instructions, put all the ingredients through a juicer and serve with or without ice.
	Calories: 173	Calories: 251	Calories: 74

Week 5

Timing	Monday/Wednesday/Friday	Tuesday/Saturday	Thursday/Sunday
Breakfast	Ingredients Beetroot, peeled - ½ Carrot - ½ Pineapple - ½ cup Lemon - ½	Ingredients Apple - ¾ Pear - ¾ Blood orange - ¾ Fresh cranberries - ¼ cup	Ingredients Stalk celery - ½ Apple - ½ Fresh ginger - ½ -inch Lemon - ¼
	Preparation Following the manufacturer's instructions, put all the ingredients through a juicer and serve with or without ice.	Preparation Following the manufacturer's instructions, put all the ingredients through a juicer and serve with or without ice.	Preparation Following the manufacturer's instructions, put all the ingredients through a juicer and serve with or without ice.
	Calories: 111	Calories: 273	Calories: 87
Dinner	Ingredients Beet - 1 Apple - 1 Ginger - 1-inch Carrots - 3	Ingredients Curly kale - ¼ bunch Lemon - ¼ Fresh ginger - ¼ -inch Cucumber - ¼ Granny smith apple - ½ Celery stalk, whole - 1	Ingredients Strawberries - 1 ½ cup Apples - 1 ½ Carrots - 1 ½ Spinach - ½ cup
	Preparation Following the manufacturer's instructions, put all the ingredients through a juicer and serve with or without ice.	Preparation Following the manufacturer's instructions, put all the ingredients through a juicer and serve with or without ice.	Preparation Following the manufacturer's instructions, put all the ingredients through a juicer and serve with or without ice.
	Calories: 254	Calories: 84	Calories: 221

Week 6

Timing	Monday/Wednesday/Friday	Tuesday/Saturday	Thursday/Sunday
Breakfast	Ingredients Apple - 1 Kiwis - 2 Mint leaves - ¼ cup Lemon - ½	Ingredients Pineapple - ½ cup Orange - ¼ Banana - ¼ Apple - ¼ Strawberries - ¼ cup Grapes - ¼ cup	Ingredients Orange - 1 Pineapple - ½ cup Lemon - ½
	Preparation Following the manufacturer's instructions, put all the ingredients through a juicer and serve with or without ice.	Preparation Following the manufacturer's instructions, put all the ingredients through a juicer and serve with or without ice.	Preparation Following the manufacturer's instructions, put all the ingredients through a juicer and serve with or without ice.
	Calories: 270	Calories: 145	Calories: 145
Dinner	Ingredients Apple - 1 Tangerine - 1 Lemon - 1	Ingredients Peach - 1 Apricot - 1 Apple - 1	Ingredients Pineapple - ¼ Apples - ½ Orange - ½ Pear - ½ Lime - ¼
	Preparation Following the manufacturer's instructions, put all the ingredients through a juicer and serve with or without ice.	Preparation Following the manufacturer's instructions, put all the ingredients through a juicer and serve with or without ice.	Preparation Following the manufacturer's instructions, put all the ingredients through a juicer and serve with or without ice.
	Calories: 165	Calories: 192	Calories: 247

Week 7

Timing	Monday/Wednesday/Friday	Tuesday/Saturday	Thursday/Sunday
Breakfast	Ingredients Carrot - 1 Beetroot - ½ Tomato - ½ Ginger - 1-inch Mint - 1 spring	Ingredients Papaya - ½ cup Pomegranate - ½ cup Guava -1 Sapota - 1	Ingredients Carrot - ½ Papaya - 4 cubes Lettuce - 2 leaves Tomato - ½ Lemon - ½
	Preparation Following the manufacturer's instructions, put all the ingredients through a juicer and serve with or without ice.	Preparation Following the manufacturer's instructions, put all the ingredients through a juicer and serve with or without ice.	Preparation Following the manufacturer's instructions, put all the ingredients through a juicer and serve with or without ice.
	Calories: 69	Calories: 248	Calories: 50
Dinner	Ingredients Tomatoes - 2 Stalk celery - ½ Cucumber - ½ Parsley - 1 handful	Ingredients Mango - 1 Passion fruits - 2	Ingredients Chives - 2 tbsp. Tomato - 1 Fresh jalapeño, seeded - 2 tbsp. Red bell pepper - ½ Stalk celery - 1 Carrot - ½
	Preparation Following the manufacturer's instructions, put all the ingredients through a juicer and serve with or without ice.	Preparation Following the manufacturer's instructions, put all the ingredients through a juicer and serve with or without ice.	Preparation Following the manufacturer's instructions, put all the ingredients through a juicer and serve with or without ice.
	Calories: 90	Calories: 237	Calories: 46

Week 8

Timing	Monday/Wednesday/Friday	Tuesday/Saturday	Thursday/Sunday
Breakfast	Ingredients Oranges - 2 Papaya - 1 cup	Ingredients Carrot - 1 Tomato - 1 Mint leaves - 1 cup Lemon - 1	Ingredients Fresh parsley - ½¼ cup Spinach - 1 ½ cups Lemon, peeled - ¼ Pear - 1 Stalks celery, trimmed - 3
	Preparation Following the manufacturer's instructions, put all the ingredients through a juicer and serve with or without ice.	Preparation Following the manufacturer's instructions, put all the ingredients through a juicer and serve with or without ice.	Preparation Following the manufacturer's instructions, put all the ingredients through a juicer and serve with or without ice.
	Calories: 235	Calories: 96	Calories: 91
Dinner	Ingredients Celery stalks - 2 Cucumber - ¼ Parsley leaf - ½ bunch Kale leaves - 1 ½ Baby spinach - ¼ handful Lime - ½	Ingredients Spinach - ¾ cup Grapefruit - ¼ Green apple - 1 Fresh ginger - ½ -inch Stalk celery - 1	Ingredients Kale - 1 cup Orange - 1 Celery stalks - 3 Cucumber - ½ Lemon juice - ½
	Preparation Following the manufacturer's instructions, put all the ingredients through a juicer and serve with or without ice.	Preparation Following the manufacturer's instructions, put all the ingredients through a juicer and serve with or without ice.	Preparation Following the manufacturer's instructions, put all the ingredients through a juicer and serve with or without ice.
	Calories: 32	Calories: 55	Calories: 158

Week 9

Timing	Monday/Wednesday/Friday	Tuesday/Saturday	Thursday/Sunday
Breakfast	Ingredients Strawberries - 5 Celery stalk - 1 Green apple - ½ Cucumber - ½	Ingredients Celery stalks - 2 Carrot - ½ Broccoli - 1 cup Apple - ½ Lemon - ¼	Ingredients Head lettuce - ½ Cucumber - ½ Spinach - ¼ cup Kale leaves - 1 ½ Lime - ¼ Green apples - 1 ½
	Preparation Following the manufacturer's instructions, put all the ingredients through a juicer and serve with or without ice.	Preparation Following the manufacturer's instructions, put all the ingredients through a juicer and serve with or without ice.	Preparation Following the manufacturer's instructions, put all the ingredients through a juicer and serve with or without ice.
	Calories: 130	Calories: 126	Calories: 231
Dinner	Ingredients Swiss chard leaves - 1 ½ Parsley - ½ cup Apple - 1 Orange - 1 Cucumber - ¼ Spinach - ¼ cup	Ingredients Carrot - 1 Tomato - 1 Cucumber - ½	Ingredients Red grapes - 1 cup Spinach - ½ cup Brussels sprouts - ¼ cup
	Preparation Following the manufacturer's instructions, put all the ingredients through a juicer and serve with or without ice.	Preparation Following the manufacturer's instructions, put all the ingredients through a juicer and serve with or without ice.	Preparation Following the manufacturer's instructions, put all the ingredients through a juicer and serve with or without ice.
	Calories: 240	Calories: 70	Calories: 116

Week 10

Timing	Monday/Wednesday/Friday	Tuesday/Saturday	Thursday/Sunday
Breakfast	Ingredients Broccoli - ½ cup Apples - 1 ½ Garlic clove - ½	Ingredients Tomato - 1 Bottle ground - 1 Ginger - ½ -inch	Ingredients Blueberries - ¼ cup Peach - 1 large Chard - ¼ cup
	Preparation Following the manufacturer's instructions, put all the ingredients through a juicer and serve with or without ice.	Preparation Following the manufacturer's instructions, put all the ingredients through a juicer and serve with or without ice.	Preparation Following the manufacturer's instructions, put all the ingredients through a juicer and serve with or without ice.
	Calories: 192	Calories: 52	Calories: 96
Dinner	Ingredients Ribs celery - 1 ½ Beet - ¼ Blueberries - ½ cup	Ingredients Pomegranate seeds - ½ cup Orange - ¼ Broccoli - 1/3 Green apple - ½	Ingredients Stalk celery - 1 Cucumber - ¼ Lime - ¼ Cilantro - ½ cup Kale - ½ cup Green apple - ½
	Preparation Following the manufacturer's instructions, put all the ingredients through a juicer and serve with or without ice.	Preparation Following the manufacturer's instructions, put all the ingredients through a juicer and serve with or without ice.	Preparation Following the manufacturer's instructions, put all the ingredients through a juicer and serve with or without ice.
	Calories: 56	Calories: 169	Calories: 93

CHAPTER 18
CONCLUSION

NAFLD is one of the main sources of liver sickness around the world. avoid the high mortality rates associated with the disease, health professionals should be on the lookout as it progresses from simple steatosis to steatohepatitis and, finally, cirrhosis. Treatment should concentrate more on managing the "insulin resistance-metabolic syndrome" than on the actual fatty liver disease. The disease's widespread recognition will make it difficult to start the necessary interventions and educate the public. Exercise and weight loss have been shown in some instances to lessen fibrosis reversion and steatosis inflammation. Vitamin E can only be used safely in adults with biopsy-proven NASH. There is ongoing discussion regarding how high fructose syrup consumption affects the emergence of NAFLD. While the data for n-3 fatty acids and probiotic supplementation are still conflicting but promising, the data for vitamin C show no discernible effect. Researchers have studied the connection between dietary habits, dietary patterns, and NAFLD extensively over the past ten years. A significant challenge in the management of NAFLD patients is nutritional research. This is crucial because NAFLD can be effectively controlled with lifestyle modifications like diet, exercise, and weight loss. Multiple characteristics of NAFLD are improved over time by calorie-restricted diets. The precise macronutrient composition of the diet appears to be less significant, despite the fact that more research is required to fully understand this issue. Low fat/high starch hypocaloric diets and high fat/low sugar hypocaloric counts calories have been demonstrated to be similarly compelling in bringing down liver lipids. The Mediterranean diet significantly reduces steatosis even in the absence of weight loss, whereas the Western diet is associated with a higher risk of NAFLD. Research on nutrition and NAFLD is significantly hampered by the disease's slow progression. To monitor histopathological endpoints, prospective long-term trials with liver biopsies are also required. In these situations, nutritional geometry could be a very useful tool for examining the connections between different dietary components, dietary nutrients, and liver health. The many facets and connections between nutritional problems and NAFLD can be understood using models. AI algorithms developed to create a customized diet for patients will also make a significant contribution. The idea that there is no one perfect diet is becoming more and more popular, with the exception of some general nutritional recommendations. In the upcoming years, patients will most likely wear gadgets that keep track of their food intake. Profound learning will handle this information and computer based intelligence will coordinate it with different information to give individualized dietary proposals and nourishing advising for the avoidance and treatment of NAFLD (actual work, anxiety, rest, microbiome, physiological constants, meds, and genome). Finally, in order to avoid fatty liver disease, we must adopt a healthy lifestyle. In this context, "maintain" refers to eating healthy foods to protect your body. We should eat a variety of foods and maintain a healthy diet. This book contains accurate information about fatty liver disease, including it's causes, symptoms, tips, foods to eat, and foods to avoid. This cookbook includes 150 recipes with carefully crafted images to aid in fatty liver disease.

BONUS: Scanning the following QR code will take you to a web page where you can access 5 fantastic bonuses after leaving your email contact: Body Fat Calculator, Body Mass Index Calculator, Daily Caloric Needs Calculator, 2 mobile apps for iOS and Android.

https://BookHip.com/VFNAWJW

REFERENCE PAGE

Detoxing Your Liver: Fact Versus Fiction. (2021, November 3). Johns Hopkins Medicine. Retrieved September 28, 2022, from https://www.hopkinsmedicine.org/health/wellness-and-prevention/detoxing-your-liver-fact-versus-fiction

Diet and Lifestyle Tips to Reverse Fatty Liver Disease. (2016, February 19). WebMD. Retrieved September 28, 2022, from https://www.webmd.com/hepatitis/fatty-liver-disease-diet

Eske, J. (2022a, September 20). What to know about leaky gut syndrome. Retrieved September 28, 2022, from https://www.medicalnewstoday.com/articles/326117

Fatty Liver Disease: Risk Factors, Symptoms, Types & Prevention. (n.d.). Cleveland Clinic. Retrieved September 28, 2022, from https://my.clevelandclinic.org/health/diseases/15831-fatty-liver-disease#:%7E:text=Fatty%20liver%20disease%20(steatosis)%20is,10%25%20of%20your%20liver's%20weight.

Johnson, J. (2021a, September 30). What to eat for a fatty liver. Retrieved September 28, 2022, from https://www.medicalnewstoday.com/articles/320082#foods-to-eat

Johnson, J. (2021b, September 30). What to eat for a fatty liver. Retrieved September 28, 2022, from https://www.medicalnewstoday.com/articles/320082#lifestyle-changes

Just a moment. . . (n.d.). Retrieved September 28, 2022, from https://onlinelibrary.wiley.com/doi/full/10.1111/liv.14360

The Liver and Its Functions | Columbia University Department of Surgery. (n.d.). Retrieved September 28, 2022, from https://columbiasurgery.org/liver/liver-and-its-functions#:%7E:text=The%20liver%20is%20the%20largest,in%20the%20right%20upper%20abdomen.

Liver Cleansing Diet. (2008, May 4). HealthEngine Blog. Retrieved September 28, 2022, from https://healthinfo.healthengine.com.au/liver-cleansing-diet#:%7E:text=The%20dietary%20recommendations%20of%20liver,focus%20on%20eating%20unprocessed%20foods.

NCBI - WWW Error Blocked Diagnostic. (n.d.). Retrieved September 28, 2022, from https://www.ncbi.nlm.nih.gov/pmc/articles/PMC4381180/

NHS website. (2022, July 1). Cirrhosis. nhs.uk. Retrieved September 28, 2022, from https://www.nhs.uk/conditions/cirrhosis/#:%7E:text=Cirrhosis%20is%20scarring%20(fibrosis)%20of,the%20liver%2C%20such%20as%20hepatitis.

SIBO (Small Intestinal Bacterial Overgrowth): Symptoms, Diet, Causes & What it Is. (n.d.). Cleveland Clinic. Retrieved September 28, 2022, from https://my.clevelandclinic.org/health/diseases/21820-small-intestinal-bacterial-overgrowth-sibo

The Healthline Editorial Team. (2021, November 11). What to Know About Fatty Liver Disease. Healthline. Retrieved September 28, 2022, from https://www.healthline.com/health/fatty-liver

What to Know About Diet After Gallbladder Surgery. (2021, June 14). WebMD. Retrieved September 28, 2022, from https://www.webmd.com/digestive-disorders/what-to-know-diet-after-gallbladder-surgery

Manufactured by Amazon.ca
Bolton, ON

32535873R00070